Californian Catholicism

The Religious Contours of California
Window to the World's Religions

A nine-volume series co-edited by
Phillip E. Hammond and Ninian Smart
DEPARTMENT OF RELIGIOUS STUDIES
UNIVERSITY OF CALIFORNIA, SANTA BARBARA

Californian Catholicism

KAY ALEXANDER

Volume I of
The Religious Contours of California
Window to the World's Religions

A PROJECT OF
The Center for the Study of Religion
University of California, Santa Barbara

IN ASSOCIATION WITH
The California Historical Society

FITHIAN PRESS

SANTA BARBARA • 1993

Design and typography by Jim Cook

Published by Fithian Press
Post Office Box 152
Santa Barbara, California 93102

LIBRARY OF CONGRESS CATALOGING-IN-PUBLICATION DATA
Alexander, Kay.
    Californian Catholicism / Kay Alexander.
        p. cm. — (The Religious contours of California: v. 1)
    Includes bibliographcal references and index.
    ISBN 1-56747-062-5
    1. Catholic Church—California—History. 2. California—
Church history. I. Title. II. Series.
BX1415.C2A44   1993
282'.794—dc20   93-14263
                                                               CIP

Contents

The Religious Contours of California

The series of books of which this volume is part is meant to engage the interest of California's citizens in the religions of their state. These range from Christian groups to Muslims, from Jews to Buddhists. They include the religions of Native Americans, of East Asian immigrants, and varieties of African American faith. The "new" religious movements of the 1960s and '70s are well represented in this state, as well as religions born in nineteenth-century America, such as Mormonism and Christian Science, and they too are part of this series. California, as is well known, is a heterogeneous society, and its religious life is likewise diverse; our series reveals just how diverse.

The series has a second purpose, however, and that is to inform readers about the world's religions. It is one thing to learn, for example, about Islam, Judaism, or Christianity as they have been and are practiced in California; it is another thing to discover where such religions originated, how they developed, and where else they currently are found. Each volume in the series therefore fits, at least loosely, a common outline. Each begins with an introduction to some religious tradition as it is found in California, then moves to an analysis of the interplay of that tradition and the state: how is California affected by the presence of this tradition, and how is the tradition affected by its presence in California? It is during this

7

analysis that the reader learns about the history and global experience of the religious tradition that is the book's focus, for in attempting to understand any spiritual tradition in California one necessarily compares the situation here with situations elsewhere. The series will be successful, then, to the degree readers find they have learned not only about a religion close at hand, but learned also about that religion worldwide.

The series arose out of a project pioneered at the University of California at Santa Barbara to help high school teachers and others understand world religions through their manifestations in California. We conceived the parallel idea of recruiting a team of authors who would be able to put together a lucid set of books to inform the general public of the ways in which this state has drawn on divergent sources of religious belief and practice in forming a multicultural and rich society. In many ways California is indeed the future.

We believe that this series will help to fulfill one of the obligations of the University of California: to bring knowledge and understanding to the citizens of this great state, and to others in America, and to return directly some of the benefits conferred on us as researchers and teachers by its tax-paying citizens. Thus, royalties from the sales of these books go not to the authors or editors but into a fund the purpose of which is the furtherance of the public's understanding of all religious traditions. We hope we can in such a way make a small contribution to a fruitful living together of diverse spiritual practices.

In all this we try to be what may be called warmly objective. The authors, as students of religion, wish to give a fair and rounded account of each religion. We are not, as scholars of religions, in the business of preaching, of course, but we wish to bring out something of the spirit of each tradition. This series is thus a contribution to the mutual understanding of religions as well as a means of giving readers an idea of California's religious variety. We are grateful to the Lilly Endowment and to the Provost at UCSB for their financial assistance in publishing the series.

PHILLIP E. HAMMOND
NINIAN SMART
Editors

Introduction

Californian Catholicism is a complex thing. It developed in the particular geographical isolation that existed in California into the twentieth century, the work of Roman Catholics coming from many states and countries. It has its historical roots in Spanish Catholicism, joined later by American Catholicism (itself a blend) and, still later, by the folk Catholicism of Mexico. These various elements have interacted in new ways in the religiously and culturally pluralistic environment of California. As a result, Californian Catholics are making important contributions to profound changes taking place in practices and beliefs of Roman Catholics worldwide.

Roman Catholicism was introduced into California by Franciscan missionaries. Recent efforts to beatify their leader, Father Junípero Serra, have resulted in two polarized camps: one promoting what is referred to as the "mission myth" of the beneficent padres and their smiling converts, the other holding the view that European-native contact in California was one of violence and bloodshed from the beginning. Chapter one attempts to get at the truth and suggests it lies somewhere in between. It also details the eventual decline and fall of the missions.

In assessing ultimate responsibility, readers should consider the consequences of the close alliance between civil and spiritual authority characteristic of New Spain (Mexico) of which California became a province. At the same time, it is also salutary to consider what might have been the consequences if either the soldiers or the padres had entered California alone or if the Native population had not been vulnerable to European diseases. As the drama actually unfolded, the Spanish Franciscans and soldiers, the Mexicans, and eventually the *Californios* (comprising Spaniards and Mexicans who intermarried with the native population as well as immigrating Yankees) all had a role to play.

North American Catholicism arrived in California with the Gold Rush and these pioneer days are discussed in chapter two. English-speaking Irish missionaries sent to the mining camps were surprised by aspects of American Catholicism, and their yearly reports sent back to Ireland present a vivid picture of their shock, and creative response, in encountering a religiously pluralistic society for the first time.

Chapter three describes Hispanic Catholicism, an influential form of Catholicism in California, which increased cultural pluralism within Californian Catholicism. Most influenced by the folk Catholicism of Central Mexico, the differences include not just ethnic customs of food and dress but, more directly, religious differences also. For example the devotion in Mexico to regional saints has parallels, though not as strong, in California Catholicism, especially in the southern part of the state. Another example is the Mexican tendency toward anti-clericalism not otherwise typical of the United States.

Folk Catholicism presents other important differences as well, such as its understanding of the nature of illness and healing and its view of the soul. Hispanic Catholic groups already resident in California recognized affinities to their beliefs as well as differences in Mexican folk Catholicism. Understanding the interaction within these groups as well as the interaction of Hispanic Catholics with other Catholics in California is important for understanding the problems and influence of a growing segment of the Catholics in the United States.

Chapter four moves to a discussion of events since Vatican II which have contributed to changing Catholic self-understandings and practices especially with regard to sexual morality. Here, again, there is no claim that this is exclusively a California phenomenon. Rather the reader is asked to consider in what ways Californians may be contributing to changing Catholic understandings of the nature of persons, and persons in relationships, and how these understandings may influence basic Catholic doctrine.

Chapter five considers the effect that religious pluralism and the challenging intellectual climate of California may be having on the beliefs of Catholics. Many Catholics are educated at the eight campuses of the University of California as well as at the twenty campuses of the California State College and University systems and the one hundred and seven California Community Colleges. In the atmosphere of free inquiry encouraged by this enveloping system of public higher education, it is inevitable that belief systems will be challenged. Further, with significant new discoveries influencing biblical studies and the post-Vatican II freedom of Catholic scholars to participate in those studies, California is nurturing scholarship of great importance to Catholics. The creative interaction of pluralism, freedom and scholarship is the subject of the final chapter.

Many students of Roman Catholic history see causal connections between the so-called "Americanist Heresy" of the nineteenth century in America and the Second Vatican Council. If such a connection exists, then American Catholicism (that is Roman Catholicism as it developed in the particular environment of the United States) had a profound influence on the worldwide Catholic Church. Are the seeds of this type of change presently being nurtured in the particular environment of California? This is one of the issues addressed—with a focus on Catholicism in California to be sure, but with attention also to the interplay of local with national and international forces.

A word about demographics. Current statistics on the Catholic population of California are taken from the *Official Catholic Directory* as of January 1, 1990. In order to interpret them, it is useful to know that, unlike some Protestant groups, Catholics do not remove members from their roles except in cases of excommunication or on personal request. To be baptized a Catholic is to be always counted as a Catholic, no matter how lapsed.

A word, also, about terminology. The terms "American Catholicism" and "Californian Catholicism" are not intended to indicate entities existing outside the Roman Catholic Church. Rather, they are meant to indicate complexes of belief and practice which have developed within Roman Catholicism in the context of a particular set of circumstances. This study is designed to explore the circumstances involved in the development of "Californian Catholicism" against the background of the development of the state.

The term "scholars" at no time refers to all scholars. There are few assertions when it comes to religion to which all scholars would assent. Rather "scholars" refers to those individuals who are studying and dealing with the most up-to-date information available in their various areas of study and are part of the present consensus in their fields.

Catholic theologians discriminate between the Jesus of history and the Christ of Faith, in Christian theology terms applying to the same person. Scholars look to the books and letters collected in the New Testament as their best source for understanding the historical Jesus even as they agree that history was already being refracted through the theological perspectives of their authors.

The Christ of Faith is of particular importance to Catholics because their theology holds that He has been present in Spirit and working in the midst for almost two thousand years and that they, alone, correctly preserve the history of this work in their teaching, the magisterium. In this sense they understand themselves to be bearers of revealed Truth and members of the True Church. Scholars, therefore, find study of the doctrines contained in the magisterium to be important for understanding the Christ of Faith preserved and transmitted by Catholics.

The term "Catholic," when it appears unmodified in this study, refers to "Roman Catholic," the largest of the Catholic groups. The second largest, the Eastern Orthodox Catholics, are also present in California but their story must remain for another time. An interesting feature of the religious pluralism of California is that various groups which became schismatic in the early centuries of the development of Christianity have been geographically reunited in California.

A final word about the "unblushing naturalism" of Californians given early mention by a Catholic bishop in chapter two, and the pervasive secularism of American society that raises its head in chapter four. These concepts relate in an interesting way in California.

"Naturalism," understood as enjoying the gifts of nature, has been present in California from the beginning. Consider the early Spanish navigator who believed the Natives to be hopelessly uncivilized because they spent hours lying naked, motionless and face down in the sun. What might he think today if he sailed past the Southern California beaches? Or take the case of Richard Henry Dana who, before the Gold Rush, reported favorably from California to New England on the freedom enjoyed in personal relationships—a type of "unblushing naturalism" built into the California Dream from the beginning.

"Secularism"—the view that there is no absolute Truth, no purpose in the universe, and no absolute moral demands—is a more recent arrival. Note that the antidote suggested to both "unblushing naturalism" and "secularism" is religious experience or "spirituality." Many have found California singularly equipped to provide this type of experience. How they have explored California's possibilities, and how Catholics have participated in and related to these efforts, is part of the story of the development of Californian Catholicism.

Some years ago, the noted Catholic historian, Father Thomas T. McAvoy, observed that, with an important exception, during the late nineteenth century the most important region affecting the social and cultural progress of American Catholicism was east of the Rockies. "California," McAvoy noted, "was an exception to this trend, as it was an exception to most of the trends of the country." The following pages attempt to spell out what McAvoy meant by this as well as detail how Californian Catholics have contributed to the reputation of California as an exception—a trend setter and a trend breaker—in the twentieth century.

1 Franciscan Roots

*Go, Fathers and dearly beloved Brethren, with the blessings of
God and of our Father St. Francis, to labor in the mysterious
vineyards of California which our Catholic sovereign has confided
to our care.*

  —The Father Guardian of the College of San Fernando in
Mexico City to Junípero Serra and his fellow missionaries, 1767

The supreme head of the Roman Catholic Church, the Pope in
Rome, had good reason, in 1763, to study his maps locating the
Catholic faithful around the world. With the end of the Seven
Years War and the cession by Catholic France to Protestant England of most of France's claims to vast territories in North America,
the balance of power between Catholics and Protestants had
shifted. To England had gone the French territory west of the thirteen English colonies as far as the Mississippi River, as well as the
city of New Orleans on its west bank. In addition, the vast territory
north of the Great Lakes, eventually to become Canada, fell to England. Catholic Spain received the French Louisiana territory
(except New Orleans) lying west of the Mississippi to act as a
buffer between New Mexico, the most northern colonial province

of New Spain, and the North Americans pushing west from the Atlantic seaboard.

The maps in the Vatican showed Santa Fe, capital of New Mexico, with its Palace of the Governors built in 1610 and, north of Santa Fe, San Fernando de Taos settled by French Catholic fur trappers. To the south and southwest of Santa Fe they showed numerous Native American tribes and Catholic missions in the provinces of New Mexico, Chihuahua, and Sonora but north and west of these settlements maps faded into whiteness.

Along the far western coast of the continent, maps indicated scattered villages on the long lower peninsula, a few ports and islands up the coast, and Russian settlements far to the north. A mighty fresh-water bay, reported by captains of the Manila Galleons to lie north of Monterey Bay, had been relegated to fable. However, the entire coast and the unexplored territory stretching inland to the Rocky Mountains had been claimed by Spain and had been named. Maps identified it as "California."

Charles III, King of Spain and the best informed of European monarchs about the New World after two and a half centuries of Spanish exploration and studying his maps and charts in the same year, would have confronted the same vast territory of whiteness labeled "unexplored." He was aware, however, that the Russians as well as the English were interested in establishing claims bordering on his territory. His response to their threatening presence on his colonial frontiers was a resolve to protect Spanish interests by building a chain of forts stretching from Louisiana to the Pacific. In their resolve to protect their power, the Pope in Rome and the King in Spain found a common cause.

Two and a quarter centuries later the result of this joint resolve has a vast legacy. In 1990, there were 7,114,514 Roman Catholics living in California, being served by 24 bishops and 3,965 priests in 1,065 parishes. They represented approximately 13 percent of the Roman Catholics living in the United States. The Archdiocese of Los Angeles, comprising Los Angeles, Ventura, and Santa Barbara counties, had an estimated 3.4 million parishioners, making it the largest Catholic population in the country. With 3,400 clerical and 12,000 lay employees, the Archdiocese administered a school system second in size in California only to the Los Angeles Unified District. In addition it operated ten cemeteries, five colleges, sixteen hospitals treating over a million patients a year, as well as numerous Catholic welfare agencies. This great, urban Archdiocese, which presently includes at least 65 percent of the members of all religions in its territory, has, along with the Archdiocese of San Francisco and other dioceses in the state, roots in more pastoral beginnings.

The Roman Catholic presence in California derives from the missionary labors of the Franciscans, members of the Order of the Friars Minor (OFM). The Franciscans and the Jesuits, or members of the Society of Jesus (SJ), were the two principal missionary and teaching orders to come originally to New Spain, the Spanish colony later to become Mexico. They brought with them the encompassing medieval worldview that besides heaven, the dwelling place of God and His angels, there is also the pit of the inferno which exists for all sinners who, suffering eternal damnation, must forever forsake hope of seeing God. According to Catholic doctrine, salvation from the inferno depends on the sacraments of the Church. Therefore, the early missionaries considered it their apostolic calling to take the sacraments—and most particularly the Eucharist, the central sacrament of the Mass—to the otherwise damned.

More than two centuries after their arrival in New Spain, the Franciscans continued north, building missions in Alta or Upper California. Many Californians reside in cities named after the early missions which are themselves named for Catholic saints particularly venerated by the Franciscans. Mission San Francisco de Asís honors St. Francis, the founder of the Order of the Friars Minor (the Franciscans), and Mission Santa Clara de Asís, the founder of its related sisterhood. Missions San Buenaventura, San Juan Capistrano, San Diego de Alcala, and San Francisco Solano, honor Franciscan theologians and missionaries. Missions Santa Barbara and Santa Inéz recall early virgins and martyrs, while the Church hierarchy is represented by Mission San Luis Obispo, named for a sainted Bishop of Toulouse. San Luis Rey de Francia and San Fernando Rey de España honor kings who were members of the lay Third Order of St. Francis, while Mission San Carlos Borromeo was probably named to honor Charles (Carlos) III himself.

The Mission San Antonio de Padua is named for a Franciscan son of a knight who, after Christ and the Virgin Mary, received the most popular devotion in Hispanic California, while devotion of the faithful to three great archangels is brought to mind by the missions San Miguel, San Raphael and San Gabriel. Finally, most reverently named are those missions recalling the most sacred, central symbols and persons of the Catholic faith: La Purísima Concepción de Maria Santísima, the most pure or immaculate conception of the most Holy Mary, the mother of Jesus; San José, Saint Joseph, the husband of Mary and the patron saint of California; San Juan Bautista, Saint John the Baptist who baptized Jesus at the beginning of his public ministry; Santa Cruz, the sacred cross on which he was crucified at its close; and Nuestra Señora Dolorísima de la Soledad, Our Most Sorrowful Lady of Solitude recalling Mary again in her sorrow following the crucifixion.

In the cities of the saints, visitors can see the whitewashed stone and adobe missions, both original and restored, most of which still stand as the oldest buildings in California. Originally built in great quadrangles modeled after the Mexican hacienda, with housing for the missionaries and their neophyte converts as well as workrooms for the neophyte artisans, their great central sanctuaries still serve the Catholics who enter to worship at their altars.

Three types of Roman Catholicism contributed to the development of Catholicism in California. First to arrive, Spanish Catholicism, brought in 1769 by the Franciscans, reflected the closest ties between church and state of any Catholic European country. Next, American Catholicism, developed in an atmosphere of complete separation of church and state after the American Revolution and the adoption of the Constitution of the United States, arrived in California with statehood in 1850. Finally, Mexican Catholicism, a unique form of folk Catholicism influenced by the ancient religions of Mexico, was brought by immigrants from central and southern Mexico to California, and since about 1910 has become a major force in shaping Hispanic Catholicism. Spanish, American, and Mexican Catholicism, in dynamic interaction, have made Californian Catholicism what it is today.

The roots of the California mission system lie in Spanish

Catholicism and the colonization of New Spain. After the arrival of Christopher Columbus in the Caribbean, Spain and Portugal fought over the right to colonize the New World. Pope Alexander VI negotiated a settlement that resulted in the division of the globe into two hemispheres. Each country was given the right to explore, colonize and establish missions in its particular half. The dividing line sliced through the eastern portion of South America, giving to Portugal the Far East, Africa, and what is now a portion of Brazil as a mission territory; to Spain went the rest of the South American continent as well as the Caribbean Islands and all of North America. However, because the Philippine Islands were first made known to Europeans by a Spaniard, Magellen, they were developed as the most Catholic territory in the Far East by Spanish missionaries, an act contested by Portugal until it was united with Spain in 1580.

Spanish Catholicism, as it was transmitted to the New World, was decisively shaped by the *Patronato Real de las Indias* of 1508, a concession whereby the popes ceded to Spanish monarchs the power and obligation to provide for the temporal maintenance of religious activities in the New World. The power granted by the *Patronato* was almost complete. A royal ordinance was required to build churches, monasteries, and hospitals, and the clerics building them required a royal license to be in the New World. The monarch recommended appointments to the Church hierarchy and the recommendations were observed by the Pope. The bulls and briefs of the Pope, as well as the decisions of diocesan and provincial councils in the New World, had to be examined and approved by the Council of the Indies, the royal council in charge of the colonies, before being published or enforced. In later centuries, new Latin American states insisted that the rights of royal patronage be passed to them as part of the sovereignty transferred by the Spanish monarchs to the new republics.

Under the provisions of the *Patronato*, the Roman Catholic Church and the Spanish monarchy worked together to colonize New Spain after its conquest by Hernando Cortés in 1519. During early colonization, the church was bound by the rule that its hierarchy, like the viceroy and his governors, had to be Spanish-born, which led to a class system. Members of the top class were

Spaniards born in Spain who went out to govern the colonies and the Church and then returned. A second class was composed of native-born Spaniards who did not return, known as *criollos* (creoles), who amassed great estates but could not rise to the top echelons of power. At a third level there rapidly developed a class of *mestizos*, part Spaniard and part Native American, who could own private property but who, in most cases, did not have the same access to education and power as the Spanish and the *criollos*. Related to the *mestizos* were the *mulattos*, individuals who traced part of their ancestry to Africa. These classes, together, came to be termed the *gente de raisón*, the people of reason, which referred during the period of the settlement of Alta (Upper) California, to people who spoke Spanish and lived like the Spanish.

At the bottom were the members of the various native populations, living in villages surrounded by common lands, which they could not sell. Some were workers with the status of serfs on great *haciendas*; their population dropped from 30 million to 6 million during the first century of colonization as great epidemics of European diseases swept the land. Their status was established by a code issued by Charles V of Spain in 1543 in response to the abuse and enslavement of the native peoples in Hispaneola (now the Dominican Republic and Haiti) and Cuba.

Under the code, known as the *New Laws of the Indies*, the native groups were permitted to dwell in their own communities and choose their leaders. Holding one of their members as a slave was forbidden. They were forbidden to dwell outside their villages; Spaniards could not stay within them for more than three days, and then only if they were merchants or if they were ill. Finally, the New Laws directed that they were to be instructed in the Catholic faith.

New Spain had experienced more than two centuries of colonization and missionary activity when Charles III responded to the growing threat of England and Russia to the northern territory claimed by Spain by sending Don José Gálvez in 1765 as visitador general to New Spain. An early problem faced by Gálvez and the Spanish viceroy was the need to provide new leadership for the Jesuit missions in Sonora, Sinaloa, and Lower California after the expulsion of the Jesuits from New Spain in 1767, brought about partly by the growing distrust on the part of European monarchs of the powerful order that was directly responsible to, and only to, the Pope.

After requesting that the Franciscans take over the Jesuit missions, Gálvez devised a plan which involved their moving north. He decided the best way to protect the border colonial provinces and Spanish interests in the Pacific was to strengthen the Spanish presence in Alta California and, to do this, he decided the territory should be colonized. Lacking available colonists who wished to emigrate from New Spain, he determined that *presidios* (forts) with adjacent missions should be established to convert the native population into loyal Spaniards.

Gálvez drew up plans for the missions in Alta California that, modeled on the New Laws, included provisions requiring native inhabitants to live in fixed domiciles in well ordered *pueblos* (towns), work in the fields, and be given their own property to cultivate to raise food for themselves. They were to be supported by the missions to which they belonged and were to dress like the *gente de raisón*. The Spanish plan provided that the missionaries would be responsible for law and order on the mission lands until the missions were converted to pueblos and the mission property turned over to its native inhabitants. The Spanish-born Franciscans connected to the apostolic College of San Fernando near Mexico City were asked to take responsibility for the establishment of the Alta California missions.

Father Junípero Serra, a member of the College of San Fernando, had already been appointed head of the Baja California missions earlier established by the Jesuits and supported by a church endowment collected by them called the Pious Fund for the Californias. He was next put in charge of the projected missions in Alta California, and missionaries were chosen to assist him, including Fathers Francisco Palou and Juan Crespí, both of whom had come to Mexico with Serra seventeen years earlier from Spain. Father Fermín Francisco Lasuén, who was to succeed Serra as president of the missions upon Serra's death in 1784, was also part of the first missionary group.

Gálvez projected four concurrent expeditions to Alta California for the purposes of exploration and mission colonization, two proceeding by land and two by sea. They were to unite in San Diego, which had earlier been charted by Sebastian Vizcaíno, and press on to Monterey. Three missionaries were chosen to accompany each of the two packet boats, and Crespí was appointed to accompany the first of the land expeditions. Serra and the recently appointed Governor of the Californias, Gaspar de Portolá, joined forces on the lower peninsula of *Baja* (Lower) California. Portolá, accompanied by fifty soldiers, and Serra, with sixteen missionaries, moved north using the established missions as their bases. In 1768, Serra founded Mission de San Fernando de Velicatá, the only mission in Baja California to be founded by Franciscans. As the most northerly of the Baja missions, it served as the jumping-off point for explorations into Alta California.

The first land expedition left Velicatá on March 24, 1769, and arrived in San Diego fifty-two days later. Serra arrived with the second land expedition, and on July 16 he erected a brushwood shelter and planted a wooden cross in front of it, thus establishing the first Roman Catholic Church in Alta California. Portolá and his men, accompanied by *neophytes* (native converts) from the Baja missions, continued north searching for Monterey Bay, which they failed to recognize though they were carrying a detailed description left by Vizcaíno.

It was not until the following year that Portolá, accompanied by Crespí, successfully located Monterey Bay, on the shore of which Serra subsequently founded Mission San Carlos Borromeo. Portolá, after supervising the building of a palisade fort and a few huts, turned over command of the territory to his lieutenant, Pedro Fages, and departed, never to return to Alta California. The San Carlos Mission was moved in 1771 to the banks of the Carmel River near the reputed site on which the Carmelites had celebrated mass with Vizcaíno in 1602. The earlier mission building became the chapel for the presidio at Monterey and is still in use. Mission San Carlos Borromeo in Carmel became the Franciscan headquarters and the final resting place of Serra when he died in 1784.

The following year two additional missions were founded. The first was built in Northern California at the base of the Santa Lucia Mountains near the present King City and dedicated to San Antonio de Padua. The second, named San Gabriel de Temblores after earthquakes experienced in the vicinity, became one of the principal missions in the vicinity of Los Angeles. The San Gabriel mission had an inauspicious beginning when soldiers cut off the head of a native chief and attached it to a fence in front of the mission. Serra attributed the initial lack of conversions at the mission to the soldiers' conduct, which continued to be a problem at other missions throughout the period of Spanish settlement.

Serra had earlier complained to the viceroy in Mexico that there was no mission named for St. Francis, the founder of the Franciscan order, and the viceroy is reputed to have replied, "If our Father San Francisco wants a mission dedicated to him, let him show us that good port up beyond Monterey, and we will build him a mission there." In response to the viceroy's challenge, Fages, Portolá's lieutenant, led an exploration north from Monterey and found the Bay of San Francisco in 1772.

Mission San Luis Obispo was established in the same year. Also in 1772 Serra, by then sixty years of age, made an arduous trip with a neophyte companion to Mexico City to plead for the establishment of further missions, against the opinion of Fages that they should not be built without adequate military protection. Serra was successful in having Fages replaced but was not any happier with the following governors, particularly Felipe de Neve who was the first to argue that, as governor, he should be given control over all mission crops, cattle and hides.

Following his trip, Serra was granted the right by Pope Clement XIV to administer the sacrament of confirmation for a period of ten years. There was a precedent for this because the right to administer this sacrament, normally a perogative reserved for a bishop, had earlier been granted to the Jesuits in Baja California. However, the word that he had received the *"Facultad de Confirmor"* did not reach Serra until four years after it was granted.

One reason the news of Serra's right to confirm was so slow to travel from Mexico City was the continued lack of a safe overland route to California. In 1774 Captain Juan Bautista de Anza, with the help of a mission neophyte, had surveyed a possible land route from Mexico City to Monterey. The following year he had led a pioneering party of more than 200 persons—including soldiers and their families, colonists, and cattle drivers—overland through Sonora by way of the Colorado River for the purpose of forming a settlement at San Francisco where the viceroy had given orders for a presidio and mission to be built. But the Anza route remained hazardous and was mostly abandoned, not to be reopened until well into the next century.

The mission of San Francisco de Asís was founded in 1776 by Palou. It was located three miles inland from the bay near a pond which Anza had named for Nuestra Señora de los Dolores, Our Lady of Sorrows, and became known as Mission Dolores. Eighteen soldiers came overland from Monterey with their wives and children to man the adjacent presidio and they became the first settlers. They were joined by settlers from the Anza colony to make an early settlement of 150 people.

By the time Serra began a tour of the missions for the purpose of confirming the neophytes, a privilege which the president of the California missions was to enjoy until 1803, the chain had grown to also include Mission San Juan Capistrano, founded in 1776 in the south, and Santa Clara, founded in 1777 in the north. The mission of San Juan Capistrano was later to see the erection of a magnificent stone church, the largest and most handsome church in California, until it came crashing down in the great earthquake of 1812. The mission at Santa Clara, located in a fertile agricultural valley south of San Francisco, became the most important in that territory.

Meanwhile, in Mexico City, the subjects of management and eventual status of the missions were being discussed more frequently. Because the Franciscans considered themselves to be holding the mission establishments in trust for their native converts, they took the position that the missionary fathers should maintain full control, using the profits that accrued from the mission estates to attract additional neophytes from the native populations. The Spanish government, on the other hand, continued to push to have the mission establishments converted into pueblos with their sanctuaries turned into parochial churches. They envisioned villages with native populations loyal to the Spanish crown served by a secular clergy under a diocesan form of church organization.

As a move toward secularization of the missions, the Spanish government recommended to Pope Pius VI that he create a diocese comprising the provinces of Sonora, Sinaloa, and both Baja and Alta California. The Pope established the diocese on May 7, 1779, thus bringing the Franciscan missions within defined canonical boundaries for the first time. However land communication remained difficult and the Bishop of Sonora, who was never to set foot in California, appointed Serra and his successors as vicars for his far-flung responsibilities in California.

With the delay of secularization, the governments in Mexico City and Spain became increasingly unwilling to rely exclusively on the Franciscans for their colonizing efforts. When Felipe de Neve was sent as governor to California, he was instructed by the viceroy to consider the feasibility of founding pueblos. After traversing the territory in 1776, de Neve recommended two sites, one in the north and one in the south. Following his recommendations, the pueblo of San José de Guadalupe, named for the patron saint of California, was founded in 1777 by presidio soldiers and colonists from Monterey and San Francisco. In 1781, the Pueblo de Nuestra Señora La Reina de Los Ángeles was founded by colonists recruited in Sonora and Sinaloa.

Gálvez had planned that the first establishments should be two forts with adjacent missions at San Diego and Monterey, with a third mission named for San Buenaventura located in between on the shore of the Santa Barbara Channel. Mission San Buenaventura still remained to be established. The viceroy in Mexico City, who continued to press for pueblo status for the missions, conceived of a new plan of organization for the native Chumash of that territory. Following his orders, de Neve met with Serra in 1782 and directed that the Chumash were not to be gathered into a mission but were to remain in their neighboring *rancherías* where the missionaries would instruct them in religion, crafts, trades, and self-government.

The missionaries opposed this plan and, when the governor proceeded up the coast to make plans for a presidio at Santa Barbara, Serra chose to ignore his directions in building the Ventura mission. Subsequently, when the presidio was founded at Santa Barbara, de Neve refused to permit Serra to found a mission in connection with it because of his insubordination.

In the meantime, the plan was tried in connection with the establishment of a mission on the Colorado River. At this mission the missionaries and soldiers were massacred by the Colorado River tribe of Yumas. As a result the plan was dropped and Lasuén, who followed Serra as president of the missions, used the old system in founding two remaining missions in the Chumash territory: Mission Santa Bárbara in 1786, the only mission to remain under uninterrupted Franciscan control to the present, and Mission La Purísima on the present site of Lompoc in 1787.

Pedro Fages returned as governor and he strongly urged further colonization to protect California. He informed the viceroy that with more neophytes moving onto the mission lands, the missionaries had more mouths to feed and could not be relied upon to provide supplies for the presidios. In 1787, Captain Nicholas Soler, Inspector General of presidios, expressed the view that the neophytes should be released from the missions, that Spanish settlers should be allowed to settle on mission lands, and neophytes permitted to settle on Spanish town lands. Fages responded to Soler with arguments which would be used again at the time of final secularization. He said that the neophytes were not ready and that the Laws of the Indies prevented Spanish settlement on mission lands because they were eventually to belong to the neophytes.

Further missions continued to be built and Lasuén helped the mission fathers replace the earlier buildings built of brush and mud with imposing stone and adobe structures. Mission Santa Cruz, founded in 1790 by Lasuén, experienced difficulties because of its proximity to undesirable settlers in the colony of Branciforte, a colony established on the present site of the city of Santa Cruz which eventually failed. Colonists could not be persuaded to come to Alta California from New Spain and the government resorted to sending convicts as settlers beginning in 1791. La Soledad, founded in 1791, also experienced difficulties and did not thrive.

In 1796, Diego Borica arrived as governor, and Lasuén conferred with him about the possibility of establishing five more missions which would permit travelers to find one as a stopping point each night of their journey along the *Camino Real* (King's Highway). Borica wrote to the viceroy, who concurred, and in 1797 five additional missions were founded: San José, about fifteen miles north of the pueblo, established twenty years earlier; San Juan Bautista, founded thirteen days later, also in the north; San Miguel Arcángel, located halfway between San Luis Obispo and San Antonio de Padua; and, in the south, San Fernando Rey de España, near the pueblo of Los Angeles, as well as San Luis Rey de Francia, which became the largest and richest of the missions.

With the exception of the two missions founded in connection with Mission Dolores—namely San Rafael, originally an *asistencia* or branch, founded in 1817, and San Francisco Solano, established without prior governmental permission as a replacement for Mission Dolores in 1823—Mission Santa Ynéz, founded in 1804 to serve the neophytes living over the mountains from Santa Barbara, was the last to be founded. San Rafael was intended to be a sanitarium for neophytes made unhealthy by the damp and foggy location of Mission Dolores. Native Americans had no immunity to European diseases, which were the major cause of the shrinking of the native populations both in and out of the missions.

During this foundational period, the missions of California had remained isolated and remote from great events that were taking place beyond their borders. The revolution of the thirteen English colonies in 1776 and their subsequent confederation into the United States of America had caused hardly a ripple in California. Neither was much notice taken of the organization by the Americans of their western territories stretching to the Mississippi and their plans for how these territories would eventually become additional states. In 1789 the French Revolution was similarly ignored. But in 1803 France sold the Louisiana Territory to the United States for $15 million, thereby doubling the size of the new republic. Suddenly, westward-moving Americans were on the Spanish frontier of New Mexico, exploring the vast territory to its north.

Americans moved rapidly into Louisiana and Missouri mingling with the Catholic French who had earlier settled there as colonists. Traders and fur trappers began to move across the plains on the 800-mile Santa Fe trail lying between Missouri and Santa Fe. In 1804 Meriwether Lewis and William Clark were sent by President Thomas Jefferson into the territory north of the Spanish missions and west of the Rocky Mountains. Their explorations provided a basis for American claims to that territory that competed with those of Spain and England.

Even the conquest of Spain by Napoleon Bonaparte, which resulted in a republican government under a *cortés*, or parliament, was a remote event in California. As liberals and conservatives battled in Spain, the liberal Spanish constitution of 1812, which made the Native American equal to the Spaniard, was enacted, repealed, and then reenacted in 1820. It, like the order by the *cortés* in 1813 to secularize the missions, was ignored until 1820 when Governor Pablo Vicente Solá tried to put its provisions into effect just as Spain was losing its control of California.

More notice was taken by the *Californios* in 1819 when Spain surrendered to the United States her claims to territory in the Pacific Northwest in partial exchange for the surrender by the United States of its claim to the territory of Texas because, the *Californios* noted, Americans continued to move into Texas and settle.

Meanwhile, in 1810, a revolution had begun in New Spain led by Padre Miguel Hidalgo y Costilla, a *criollo* priest who sought to liberate Mexico from the control of the Spaniards. The first impact on Alta California was that as supply ships, pay for the soldiers, and revenue from the Pious Fund for the missionaries ceased to come, the support of the presidios and settlers was shifted to the missions, which were forced to become increasingly self-sufficient.

The mission neophytes' artisan skills had long been in demand wherever soldiers and settlers congregated at presidios or pueblos. In 1819, when the colonists of Los Angeles wished to replace their small adobe chapel built in 1784 with a larger church, neophytes from San Gabriel and San Luis Rey did most of the work. They were paid a *real* (12.5 cents) a day each, with the missions receiving the money. After contributions from the settlers ran out, contributions to the building fund in the form of cattle, mules, brandy, and wine arrived from the missions.

This barter economy was maintained because even though the missions richly produced wheat, hides, tallow, wool, wine, brandy, oil, olives, soap, cotton and hemp, the Spanish government did not permit foreign trade or encourage foreigners to land in colonial ports. The Spanish were coming to fear foreigners arriving from the newly formed United States as well as from their old enemies, England and Russia, and not without reason. As early as 1789, the viceroy in Mexico City reported to his successor that American colonists seemed most interested in establishing themselves on the northern coast of California. More and more Americans arriving by ship engaged in hunting and clandestine trading during the next quarter century.

During this period Russia was also on the move. In 1802 a newly formed Russian-American company, engaged in the fur trade, sent secret orders to its manager, Alexander Baranov, to push settlements as far down the northwest coast as possible to provide bases for the possible extension of Russian influence into the East Indies.

The Russian Orthodox Church, affiliated with the Eastern Orthodox churches, which had been in schism from Roman Catholicism since 1054, was the established church in Russia. In 1812, the Russians established Fort Ross north of Bodega Bay and introduced Eastern Orthodox Catholicism, with its Greek rite, into California for the first time.

There was some commerce with Lima, Peru, also a Spanish dependency, and some contact with smugglers, coming by sea from as far as Boston and China for the coveted pelts of the sea otters; but California remained remote from the Mexican mainland. Prior to the Mexican war for independence, each year two ships arrived from San Blas in Lower California with supplies and they returned with a small cargo, mostly wheat; but that was all the commerce the Spanish had permitted for the territory.

The economy of California during this period became completely dependent on the produce of the missions and the skilled labor of its neophytes. John Gilroy—who was ill with scurvy and left behind by his ship in Monterey in 1814 and who, on converting to Catholicism, was the first English-speaking foreigner permitted to remain in California—observed the following in his later reminiscences about the missions at the time of his arrival.

> The friars had everything their way. The governor and the military were expected to do whatever the friars requested. The missions contained all the wealth of the country. There was not a sawmill, whipsaw or spoked wheel in California. Such lumber as was used was cut with an ax. Chairs, tables and wood floors were not to be found except in the governor's house. Plates were rare unless that name could be applied to the tiles used instead. Money was a rarity. There were no stores and no merchandise to sell. There was no employment for a laborer. The neophytes did all the work, and all the business of the country was in the hands of the friars.

The Mexican war for independence ended in 1821 and, when the news reached California the following year, the Mexican flag was raised over the presidio at Monterey. The Mexicans, however, inherited the same problems with respect to their remote province of California that had plagued the Spanish. Moreover, they were aware that the Russian settlement at Ross was organized like a military base and rumors were rife that Spain had secretly ceded California to Russia before Mexican independence was achieved.

In December of 1823, President Monroe announced the historic doctrine that the United States would not permit further foreign colonial establishments in the western hemisphere. At the same time American fur trappers and traders continued to pour into the Pacific Northwest as well as into the Mexican border provinces of New Mexico and Sonora. After 1825, great wagons began to roll across the old Santa Fe Trail and westward moving Americans found New Mexico to be more accessible to them by land than the distant province of California was to Mexico. Under pressure from both Russia and the United States, Mexico came to the same conclusion that Spain had come to earlier, namely, that in order to protect it, it was necessary to colonize California with citizens loyal to itself.

With Mexican independence, the restrictive trade laws were relaxed, and Americans began to arrive by sea, many on the ships that came for hides and tallow. The Mexican Congress of 1824 established liberal colonization policies that permitted foreigners to obtain grants of public land not exceeding eleven leagues, providing the permanent resident was willing to be baptized and embrace the state religion of Roman Catholicism. In 1828 a naturalization law allowed a foreigner to become a naturalized citizen if the applicant had resided at least two years in the territory and had become a Roman Catholic. This law further required that to acquire land, a colonist must settle on it and cultivate it. Many Americans took advantage of these changes and became naturalized Mexican citizens while, through privileges of dual citizenship, they remained citizens of the United States.

The mission lands were extensive and fertile and, at their peak, it is estimated between 20,000 and 30,000 neophytes took care of the herds of cattle and horses, the gardens and vineyards. As newly arriving colonists looked for land on which to settle, they found that a settler required the permission of the neighboring mission to acquire land, and in places the mission lands were almost contiguous with little land in between. Settlers arriving at the pueblo of Los Angeles, for example, found that in its neighboring fertile valley, the twenty-four ranches of the San Gabriel mission contained about 1.5 million acres stretching from the ocean to the San Bernardino mountains. Other missions had been located with equal care in the most promising areas for farming and cattle ranching.

When José María Echeandía arrived in 1825 with dual appointments as the first Mexican governor and military chief, he wanted the missions to remain peaceful and productive and realized that the mission Fathers were necessary if this was to be accomplished. Though most of the missionaries were Spanish-born and loyal to Spain by persuasion, the missionaries from the four most southern missions were required to take oaths of loyalty to the Mexican constitution of 1824. Others further north refused to do so. When the Mexican government decreed in 1827 that all Spaniards in California, with certain exceptions, were to be deported, the Franciscans were not on the exceptions list. However, they were permitted to remain even though all but three were Spaniards, because to have banished them would have radically disrupted the country.

Echeandía brought a plan for the secularization of the missions similar to that of the Spanish *cortés*, namely to convert the missions into pueblos. Married neophytes who had been Christians for fifteen years and were able to earn a living would receive individual home sites and garden plots. The missions were to retain sufficient land to support the neophytes not yet ready to leave. The Franciscans opposed this plan because they saw it as a first step toward neophytes losing their land.

Echeandía proposed a new plan in 1828. The missions were to become towns composed of mission neophytes, with Mexicans permitted to reside in them. Each neophyte was to receive a house lot, a farm plot of approximately eight acres, and a generous number of farm animals and tools. Undistributed land and cattle, vineyards, orchards, mills, and similar items were to be put in charge of an administrator responsible to a town council and to the Territorial Deputation, an elected body of *Californios* representing various portions of the territory.

Because of governmental turmoil in Mexico, Echeandía received no response to his plan, so he submitted it to the Territorial Deputation, which approved it in August of 1830. The *Californios* were aware that the Mexican government had, in 1824, made mission lands exempt from colonization. A committee of the Deputation had subsequently recommended that irrigable lands not being cultivated by the missions should be given to individuals for this purpose and that interior lands should be opened to settlement.

Echeandía sent a new version of his plan to Mexico in 1830 with the provisions that only two missions, San Gabriel and San Carlos, were to to be converted into towns at first and that schools would be set up in these towns to teach the Native Americans reading, writing, and arithmetic. He issued this new version as his secularization decree of January 6, 1831, but officials in Mexico felt it did not go far enough to satisfy the Spanish secularization law of 1813.

Meanwhile, newly arriving settlers and more established colonists were casting increasingly covetous eyes on the richly spreading fields of wheat, the hills covered with cattle, and the gardens, orchards, and vineyards which surrounded the missions. They began to see possible opportunities in the new Mexican land laws and to see themselves as having a common cause. Their ranks, particularly in Northern California, were reinforced by the fur trappers who began to come overland to California after Jedediah Smith charted a route through the Utah territory with the aid of two mission neophytes in 1826.

Back in Mexico City, threatened by the questionable loyalty of its Spanish-born residents and the newly arriving foreigners, and by concern that Spain had not yet granted formal recognition to Mexican independence, the leaders of the fledgling Mexican republic conceived of two new plans for maintaining their grip on Upper California. The first involved the transfer of control of the missions from Spaniards to Mexicans with the goal of final secularization; the second, a major colonization effort by Mexicans.

In 1831, the Franciscan Apostolic College of Nuestra Señora de Guadalupe at Zacatecas, the members of which were Mexican born, was asked to send missionaries to Alta California on a fact-finding expedition with the eventual goal of taking over management of the missions. At the same time the second plan, colonization of Upper California by Mexicans, was set in motion by José María Híjar assisted by José M. Padrés. Padrés described California to prospective settlers as a Garden of Eden and, as an inducement to colonists, promised a division of the missionary property between them and the use of the neophytes as servants.

In the autumn of 1832 Father García Diego y Moreno and a small band of Zacatecans sailed from San Blas on the same ship carrying the newly appointed governor for California, José Figueroa. When they arrived in Monterey on January 15, 1833, García Diego met immediately with Father Narciso Durán, Father President of the Missions, and it was agreed that the Zacatecan missionaries would assume direction of the eight northern missions while the southern missions would remain under the control of the Spanish-born Fernandinos.

In July of 1833, Figueroa published an order for the gradual release of the neophytes from the jurisdiction of the missions. In August, the Mexican Congress directed that the missions were to be removed from the control of the Franciscans and placed under the care of the secular clergy. In April of the following year, two pieces of supplementary legislation decreed all missions were to be converted into parish churches and the mission lands were to be turned over to Híjar and his colonists.

Two hundred and fifty colonists, enlisted in Mexico City on the promise of livestock, farming equipment and land from the public domain, arrived in September of 1834. Híjar brought with him his dual appointment as governor of California and director of colonization. Meanwhile, Antonio López de Santa Anna, who had reassumed the presidency of Mexico, sent a messenger overland to Monterey with orders countermanding Híjar's appointment as governor. Híjar tried to convince Figueroa that his appointment as director of colonization was not contingent on his status as governor, but Figueroa refused to turn the mission lands over to him. Híjar and Padrés were returned to Mexico City, the colony disbanded and the settlers dispersed into the nearby territory. However, the legislation secularizing the missions and placing the bulk of the mission lands under civil administrators remained. The mission ranches were ripe for settlement by the *Californios*, who eagerly sought land grants from the Mexican government.

The secularization of the missions achieved what had been the goal of the civil authorities in California from the beginning. However, instead of taking ten years to achieve, as originally projected by Gálvez, secularization was bitterly fought over for sixty-five years. Instead of resulting in citizens loyal to Spain as originally intended, or born in Mexico and clearly loyal to the Mexican government as subsequently planned, the rich mission lands were rapidly occupied by the *Californios*, an increasingly mixed group with questionable loyalties. The mission lands were rapidly dispersed through Mexican land grants and, in many cases, subsequent purchase by immigrating Americans.

The story of the Catholic Church in California in the fourteen years between 1834 and the end of the Mexican period is one of dissolution and decline. Some of the missionaries returned to Mexico while most of the neophytes faded away. The *criollo* Zacatecans had not been well received by the *Californios*, who perceived their Mexican loyalties to be at odds with their own. When the remaining missionaries died, no new padres arrived to replace them.

In 1840, Rome attempted to curb the disaster by creating the Diocese of the Californias with the Zacatecan García Diego y Moreno as its first bishop. The Mexican government promised to release the revenues from the Pious Fund for support of the new diocese but the money was never sent. When Bishop García Diego arrived, he was identified with Mexican interests in the territory by the increasingly independent *Californios* and was widely distrusted.

Without funds and without the support of many of the Catholics in his Diocese, García Diego fought a losing battle. He first established his headquarters in San Diego because it was most accessible to both Alta and Baja California. However, San Diego was also a center of much of the seditious plotting going on in Southern California. He soon removed himself to Santa Barbara which he correctly identified as being the most Catholic of the California communities, partly because its mission remained the headquarters for the Franciscans in California. Here, again, he received a cold reception. On one occasion his carriage was overturned and he was allowed to remain pinned under it for several hours before being rescued.

The few Franciscans who remained ministered to the faithful and buried their dead adjacent to the crumbling missions, which had been the site of their apostolic endeavors. Between 1769 and 1845, the missionaries provided the sacrament of baptism to about 99,000 persons. The neophytes also buried their dead. In the same period the Franciscans gave the final sacraments and Christian burial to 74,000 persons, mostly neophytes. By the time the Bureau of Catholic Indian Missions was established in 1873, the communities of mission neophytes had shrunk to about 3,000.

As the Spanish and Mexican periods of the Catholic Church in California passed into history, a new beginning was being formed. Irish Catholic immigrants were among the first to endure the hardships of those who sought to come overland to California in the 1840s. They were joined by Italian Catholic merchants and political refugees. With the independence of California from Mexico and its acceptance two years later by the United States as the thirty-first state to join the union, the center of Catholic population shifted from Southern to Northern California. Californian Catholicism entered into a new phase as it became an integral part of American Catholicism and developed in the Gold Rush country as a pioneer church.

FURTHER READING:
Engelhardt, Zephyrin, O.F.M. *The Franciscans in California.* Harbor Springs, Michigan: Holy Childhood Native American School, 1897.
Geiger, Maynard, J., O.F.M. *Palou's Life of Fray Junípero Serra.* Washington: Academy of American Franciscan History, 1955.
Guinn, J.M. *A History of California,* Vol. I. Los Angeles: Historic Record Co., 1915.
Hutchinson, C. Alan. *Frontier Settlement in Mexican California.* New Haven: Yale University Press, 1969.
Robinson, Alfred. *Life in California.* Santa Barbara: Peregrine Press, 1970.

2 PIONEER DAYS

Of the Californians it may be said, that they are bold and independent adventurers. . . . Their belief in the possibility of living for an invisible and supernatural end is quickened by their experience of the country they have come to. . . . In no part of the world is the individual more free from restraint. . . . The great spiritual dangers in California are rank infidelity and unblushing naturalism.

—Herbert Cardinal Vaughan, *Dublin Review*, 1866

It was in April of 1848 that the cry first went out, "Gold! Gold has been discovered in California!" The first find had been made in January by James Marshall at Coloma where he was building a saw mill as part of John Sutter's wilderness empire of New Helvitia. Making use of Mexico's liberal colonization policies, Sutter had acquired title to a vast tract of land and built a fort in the Sacramento Valley, earlier named by the Spanish for the central sacrament of the Catholic Church. It had become a rendezvous point for fur trappers and the earliest immigrants to arrive overland from the United States. As Europeans, Americans, Mexicans, natives of the area, and Kanakas, which Sutter had brought from the Sandwich Islands (Hawaii), mingled, Northern California developed into a very different kind of mission field.

Sutter had tried to keep the news of gold quiet so that the men building the mill would remain. He also wished to gain time to lease an additional area from the native inhabitants. However, in February the word began to leak out, and by April the news of the discovery was shouted in the streets of San Francisco. The race to the foothills of the Sierra Nevada range was on. San Francisco, San Jose, and other towns began to lose their male populations to prospecting, as buildings remained half-built, crops went unharvested, and sailing ships lay stranded in the San Francisco Bay with no crews to sail them.

In November of the same year, Bishop John Hughes of New York wrote to José de la Guerra, a leading Catholic layman in Santa Barbara, asking him seven questions and requesting that he confidentially convey his views on the status of the Catholic Church and its mission in California to the bishops of the United States. Much had happened in California and the West in the preceding three years and the Church had not remained untouched.

In 1845, *Californios* had temporarily seized control of the territorial government from Mexico and substituted Pio Pico for Manuel Micheltorena as governor. When Pico assumed control, one of his first acts was to announce that the missions, which had been placed under civil administrators in 1834, were to be sold. On May 28, 1845, the Territorial Assembly passed a decree to sell the San Rafael, Dolores, Soledad, San Miguel, and La Purísima missions in the north. The missions San Carlos Borromeo, San Juan Bautista, San Juan Capistrano, and San Francisco Solano were declared to be pueblos. Sufficient space at each of these missions was reserved for the curate's house, a church, and a courthouse, but the remaining buildings and adjacent land were ordered sold at public auction.

The other missions, with the exception of the mission at Santa Barbara, were ordered to be rented out at the option of the government. Revenues from sales and rents were to be used to defray debts of the missions, and any surplus was to be divided between conservation of Divine worship, benefits for the neophytes, and education and public beneficence.

The following year (1846) the United States had declared war against Mexico over disputed territory resulting from the annexation of Texas by the United States the previous year. When the Americans occupied California, the Church had been allowed to function without restriction and Santa Clara, San José, San Juan Bautista, and Santa Cruz missions had been provisionally returned. With the defeat of Mexico by the United States and the signing of the treaty of Guadalupe Hidalgo in February of 1848, the vast territories of the present states of California, Nevada, Arizona, Utah, Colorado, and New Mexico, stretching from the Rocky Mountains to the Pacific and north to the border of the Oregon Territory, had been ceded by Mexico to the United States. No longer did one have to be a Roman Catholic in this area in order to own land and be a citizen.

Responding to the seven questions posed by Bishop Hughes, de la Guerra painted a bleak picture. He estimated that California contained 25,000 or 30,000 Catholics, almost all Spanish-American, to whom he added 10,000 to 15,000 Christian neophytes. Bishop García Diego y Moreno, appointed when the Diocese of the Californias had been created in 1840, had died in 1846 leaving another Franciscan, José María de Jésus González Rubio, in charge of the vacant see in California. The California Catholics were being served by a mere eight priests, of whom only two were capable of giving their all to their ministry, wrote de la Guerra, the others being too old and too infirm.

The mission buildings, with the exception of those at Santa Barbara, had passed into the hands of private individuals or been rented out and were in a very ruinous state. With many of the mission churches closed for lack of ministers, their furniture and jewels had been transferred to those still in use. Finally, de la Guerra noted, income from the Pious Fund which had supported the missions, now remained in Mexico. With the exception of a tract of land set aside by Micheltorena in the Santa Ynez Valley to support a seminary for California, the Church was without resources in California.

It was the American Catholic Church headquartered in Baltimore to which González Rubio turned for support. Appeals were sent by him and others to the American bishops for aid but the American bishops in Baltimore did not have the power to interfere and could only relay the appeals to Rome. One such appeal sent in

1847 by Jonathan D. Stevenson, the U. S. military commander located in Los Angeles, began by describing the earnest desire of the people of California to be annexed to the United States. It went on to describe the situation of the Church, with only three priests available to serve the entire Southern District of California, which had a coast of some 500 miles. The northern territory was described as being in even worse condition. Education had been entirely neglected, Stevenson reported; it was very seldom he met a man that could either read or write. Concluding that he knew of no channel through which relief could flow except through the ministers of the faith the people had been taught "to venerate and live by and in which they hope to die," Stevenson appealed for aid to "rescue these people from their present ignorance and the degradation which must follow if no relief be afforded them."

Stevenson's appeal was forwarded to Rome, but meanwhile other events had occurred bringing the American Catholic Church much closer than most Californians had realized. How it got there is an interesting chapter in the history of American Catholicism, a history already two centuries in the making.

Roman Catholicism had first been brought to the American colonies by English Catholics fleeing persecution by English Protestants. Establishing themselves on land granted by the British crown to the Catholic converts, Lord Cecil Calvert and his son, the earliest American Catholics, brought with them a religious tradition and practice by then more than 1,500 years old.

All Christians, including Roman Catholics, look back to their founder, Jesus of Nazareth. He was called the Messiah, or Christ, the Greek word for "annointed." In the first century after his death, his earliest followers organized themselves into churches guided by regional bishops. As Christianity spread, the bishops, in turn, became organized into metropolitan provinces governed by archbishops. One of these archbishops, the bishop of Rome, became preeminent and eventually was referred to as the pope.

Beginning in the fourth century, the bishops and archbishops began to meet in great councils to resolve regional differences in doctrine. Not all regional differences could be resolved and, to the east and south, churches split from the authority of Rome to establish regional forms of Christianity. To the west alliances were formed between the Church and the various monarchies, while missionaries were sent into England, Ireland and northern Europe to bring Christians of an earlier persuasion, judged heretical, into conformity. In these areas, Roman Catholicism became established as the religion fully supported by the state in a close interlocking relationship of spiritual and temporal authority known as Christendom.

Colonial America was first settled by various religious groups including the Roman Catholics who settled mainly in the territory eventually to become Maryland. Smaller groups settled elsewhere in the middle Atlantic colonies. Here they were ministered to by missionary Jesuits who established themselves on farms and built small chapels which functioned as churches. After the Revolutionary War, American Catholics sought to assert their independence of foreign control. They asked Rome for permission to choose a bishop for America, the same prerogative being exercised in the Spanish colonies to the south. Permission was granted and their choice was named bishop, but the Roman hierarchy in the Vatican headquarters in Rome began to seek ways to regain greater control.

Gradually freedoms enjoyed by Catholics in America in the early republican period were eroded, freedoms such as masses in English and the right of Catholic trustees to own and administer church property. However, American Catholicism continued to develop a distinctive character in response to a developing ethnic pluralism as French Catholics fled to America after the French Revolution, and German Catholics arrived seeking land and freedom from conscription. In spite of increasing conservatism within American Catholicism, there continued to be support in the early nineteenth century for religious pluralism, religious toleration, cordial relations with Protestants, and political participation by Catholics in the new nation. In the face of growing numbers of Catholics, the bishop of Baltimore was raised to an archbishop and further bishops were appointed in his expansive province.

Meanwhile, Americans continued to move to the west. In 1818 the boundary between the United States and Canada had been set by convention between Great Britain and the United States on the line of the 49th degree north latitude as far as the Rocky Mountains.

West of the Rocky Mountains the land north of California known as the Oregon Territory was held jointly by Britain and the United States. Americans began to immigrate into the Oregon Territory in the early 1840s, and political pressure began to mount in the United States to end the joint occupation and annex the territory.

In 1846, before the question was settled, Rome erected a metropolitan see in Oregon City with the French Canadian, Francis N. Blanchet, as its first Archbishop. It was, at first, an extension of the Canadian Catholic Church, though Blanchet built on the work of Jesuit missionaries who had been sent to the Oregon Territory by the bishop of St. Louis. With the settlement of the controversy with Great Britain and the annexation of the Oregon Territory below the 49th parallel by the United States in 1846, the metropolitan see centered in Oregon City became the second province of the American Catholic Church.

In 1847, the lack of a bishop to consecrate the holy oil needed for the sacraments in California led James Alexander Forbes, British Vice Consul in Upper California, to send an urgent plea to Archbishop Blanchet to provide holy oil for California. Forbes included an assessment of the condition of the Catholic Church in California, mentioning the rapid immigration, and pleaded that "good instructors and pastors . . . such as we now hear of in Oregon" be sent.

In July of 1848, Pio Pico returned from Mexico City with the first official word that California had been ceded six months earlier to the United States. In the autumn, Father Brouillet, the Vicar General of Archbishop Blanchet, arrived in San Francisco with the charge to build a church. Unlike his priest predecessors in the area, he could speak the language of many of the new immigrants coming from the United States and Ireland. The arrival of Brouillet thus marked a major shift of Catholic focus from Southern to Northern California and from the Spanish-speaking to the English-speaking American church.

At the beginning of 1848, San Francisco had approximately 200 buildings and fewer than 1,000 inhabitants. Already, however, it had a large foreign-born population of which the Irish were the most numerous. A small Mexican congregation continued to worship at Mission Dolores but, with gold as the impetus, California became increasingly settled by persons with ties neither to Spain nor Mexico. Instead, the United States was their focus, and statehood their rapidly developing aim.

On December 11, 1848, residents of San José met and called for a constitutional convention looking toward statehood. Subsequent meetings were held in San Francisco, Sacramento, Monterey and Sonoma. Catholic *Californios* from the Mexican period were represented but they were greatly outnumbered by the more recent American settlers in Northern California. The delegates took the constitution of Iowa, which provided for equitable taxation and a good public educational system, as their model. A bill to forbid slavery passed unanimously. The constitution for California was signed and a request for statehood, without going through a period of territoriality, was forwarded to the United States Congress on October 13, 1849.

Meanwhile de la Guerra, in his letter to Bishop Hughes, suggested that an indispensable requisite for a new bishop should be proficiency in Spanish because the Catholics in California were almost all Spanish-American. His advice was heeded, and the next two bishops consecrated for California were bilingual Catalonians. But de la Guerra's assessment was substantially a Southern Californian point of view of a vanishing situation. San Francisco and the gold-mining towns springing up along the Mother Lode now appeared to be much more important for the future of Catholicism in California. It was on booming Northern California that Catholic development came to be focused.

In June of 1850, Joseph Sadoc Alemany, a Dominican who had served scattered groups in Tennessee and Kentucky, was consecrated the bishop of the Diocese of Monterey, the new name chosen for the old Diocese of the Californias. The first choice of the American bishops had declined, and Alemany, in Rome as a delegate for a meeting of his Dominican order, was summoned to the Vatican by Pope Pius IX. Years later, Alemany recalled the pontiff's words.

You are going to a wonderful land where the government respects the rights of man, where the people are understanding, where God has revealed the treasure of His infinite bounty, where men are generous, and I am sure that the Church shall not be in want. May the blessing of the Father and the Son and the Holy Ghost be upon you and California. Depart in peace.

Alemany traveled through Europe on his way back to the United States, soliciting financial support for his new diocese and recruiting priests, as well as members of the religious orders and seminarians, to assist him. He wrote ahead to the eastern United States seeking volunteers. Meanwhile, the news was received that California had been admitted as a state. On October 29, an official celebration was held with a procession in San Francisco which included a banner with thirty-one stars carried by *Californios* and a banner of blue silk reading *The China Boys* carried by members of the Chinese colony.

When Alemany arrived a month and a half later, he found that some progress in resuscitating the Church had already been made. The request of González Rubio and others for assistance and his own call for volunteers had not gone unheeded. There were thirty-three priests in the diocese to greet Alemany, of whom twelve were diocesan, seven were Franciscan, and four were Dominican. The Picpus Fathers, who were seeking to have California made an extension of their mission to the Sandwich Islands, had sent seven. The Jesuits had sent two and the Mercy Fathers one.

Father Anthony Langlois, S.J., who had come to the Oregon Territory in 1842, had been sent to San Francisco by Blanchet in the Spring of 1849 to assist Brouillet. He was serving as pastor for the newly built Church of St. Francis on Vallejo Street, on the west side of Telegraph Hill, close to the bay where Alemany found him preaching in French, Spanish, and English in the same sermon. Langlois was later to become Alemany's Vicar-General.

Fellow Jesuits, Michael Accolti and John Nobili had also arrived from the Oregon missions in 1849 and, shortly thereafter, Brouillet had been recalled. While Accolti had also been recalled to serve as a superior of his Order, Nobili had established a ministry in San José and taken up residence in the Mission at Santa Clara. Nobili had sent a letter to González Rubio requesting that the

Jesuit presence in that area be clarified and he had received a response authorizing his ministry.

By the time Alemany arrived, Nobili had assembled the first students at Santa Clara, was conducting classes, and was seeking ways to regain the dispersed property of the mission. Subsequently he was joined by other Jesuit priests displaced by the revolution in Italy of 1848, and by 1854 they formed a community of seven priests and six brothers. A second college, St. Ignatius, which was rebuilt after the earthquake of 1906 and renamed the University of San Francisco, was also established by the Jesuits.

On Alemany's arrival, he was presented by the Catholics of San Francisco with a purse of $1,350 to assist him in visiting his wide diocese, which extended from the Rocky Mountains to the Pacific. An accomplished horseman, Alemany made many long journeys to visit remote settled districts. One of Alemany's early official acts was the dedication of St. Patrick's Catholic Church in Sacramento, which, as the central access point to the gold country, was soon to have a population equal to that of San Francisco. A newspaper described the "densely crowded ceremony" and the "mitered Bishop in gorgeous vestments" with priestly attendants assisting in the solemn High Mass. The brilliant ceremony contrasted with the poverty of the bishop's tiny, two-room cottage adjacent to St. Mary's Cathedral in San Francisco.

Years later, Herbert Vaughan, a visiting English bishop, described Alemany as still living in a "miserable, dingy little house" near the area that was to develop as Chinatown.

> To the left are a number of little yards, and the back windows of the houses in which the Chinamen are swarming. Broken pots and pans, old doors, and a yellow compost, window-frames, faggots, remnants of used fireworks, sides of pig glazed and varnished, long strings of meat—God only knows what meat—hanging to dry, dog-kennels, dead cats, dirty linen in heaps, and white linens and blue cottons drying on lines or lying on rubbish—such is the view to the left.

With help from Alemany, three Dominican Sisters of Charity opened the first convent in California on April 1, 1851. The next year they opened an asylum for orphaned girls which became Mount Saint Joseph School. Later, eight Sisters of Mercy arrived opening Saint Mary's Hospital on Stockton Street in 1857.

By 1853 the Catholic population of San Francisco numbered 40,000, and there were 38 priests in the Archdiocese. Alemany encouraged the coming of teaching orders and they soon established many schools. Saint Patrick's opened in San Francisco in 1850; Bellarmine and Notre Dame High Schools in 1851 in San Jose. In 1854, Saint Dominic's was established in Benicia, and by 1860 there were Catholic schools in Marysville, Los Angeles, and other parts of the state. The Sisters of the Holy Name and the Christian Brothers arrived in 1868, the former establishing a college in Oakland and the latter establishing Sacred Heart College, which became the most popular private boys' school in San Francisco.

By 1866, a school for girls opened by the Sisters of Presentation had a thousand students. English Bishop Vaughan, on his visit, noted that this was a particularly useful service to the community because in the public schools, boys and girls attended together. Linking this practice to "precocity in vice in California [which] exceeds anything we know in England," he added that he had even heard of a college in which boys and girls were educated together and lived under the same roof. Vaughan quoted an observation from a local newspaper which he linked to California's precocity, namely "in no part of the world is the individual more free from restraint."

The newspaper attributed this freedom of restraint to the presence in California of only a small number of women and, as a consequence, the large portion of men living in either cabins or in hotels, remote from women relatives, and therefore uninfluenced by the powers of a home. In this type of community, the newspaper observed, "public opinion, which as a guardian of public morals is more powerful than the forms of law, loses much of its power." However, Vaughan concluded, the greatest "spiritual dangers in California are rank infidelity and unblushing naturalism."

Alemany shortly began to receive an important source of aid to fight California's infidelity and naturalism in the form of missionaries from Ireland, most particularly from All Hallows College in

Dublin which had been founded in 1840 to provide missionaries and priests for English-speaking Catholics dispersed around the world. A missionary soon reported to his college that the two Catholic churches in San Francisco were crowded every Sunday in spite of "the rage for dueling, the passion for gambling and the barefaced depravity (which) prevail to a frightful degree. . . ."

One of the All Hallows missionaries, Father James Largan, was sent to minister to a population centered in Napa, which he estimated, in 1858, comprised 3,000 to 4,000 people. He said Mass in the courthouse, and found his congregation to consist of "a mixture of Protestants, Catholics, Jews and Methodists, and others who consider themselves quite free to believe or not to believe."

Noting that "in this country [where] there are almost as many religions as people," Largan found the ancient rituals of Catholicism could compete very well with the camp meetings of the Campbellites and Baptists which, in his view, turned religion into ridicule. "These meetings are just dens of immorality and vice," he wrote back to Ireland, "injurious both to religion and Christian society . . . but the preachers make plenty of money and that is all they want."

The first American Governor of California, Peter H. Burnett, raised by Baptist parents in Tennessee, recorded the deep impression that Catholicism could make on the frontier, in his case in a midnight High Mass in Fort Vancouver which he attended as a spectator on Christmas Eve in 1843. "I had never witnessed anything like it before," he recalled; "the profound solemnity of the services—the intense, yet calm fervor of the worshipers—the great and marked differences between the two forms of worship." On this occasion, Burnett's "instantaneous reflection, that it was the Church claiming to be the only true Church," made a deep impression and led to his ultimate conversion to Catholicism.

At the conclusion of his visit, Vaughan carefully assessed the possibilities for conversion and spiritual renewal in California. He found a "population composed of men of keen wits, of the most varied, world-wide experiences, and drawn from countries in which they have been more or less within the reach of Catholic teaching." They are "bold and independent adventurers," he went on, "for the greater part cut off from the traditions of home and family."

Vaughan found anti-Catholic influences to be "far away" and a singular absence of prejudice against Catholicism. However, it was in the response of Californians to the land itself that he saw the most promising possibilities for spiritual renewal for, he wrote, "their belief in the possibility of living for an invisible and supernatural end is quickened by their experience of the country they have come to."

Almost half a century ago, Henry J. Walsh, S.J., provided the definitive history of the pioneer priests who were sent out to the mining towns and camps located in the midst of some of the most inspiring scenery in the state. Starting in Tuolumne and Calaveras counties and visiting the towns made famous by Mark Twain and Bret Harte, Walsh hiked the gold dust trails of the forty-niners, photographing Catholic churches still standing in Columbia, Murphy's, San Andreas, Coloma (where gold was first discovered), Grass Valley, Sawyer's Bar, Marysville, and Folsom.

After traversing El Dorado and Amador counties, through the scented redwoods and lush valleys of the Sierra Nevada western foothills, he crossed the high mountain passes to visit the desert valleys and Mono Lake country lying beyond their eastern escarpment. He returned through the Trinity Alps visiting Mount Shasta as well as the counties to the north of Marysville, eventually arriving at Sacramento. This was the missionary field of the mostly Irish missionaries of the 1850s and 1860s who came to minister to Catholics in the territory marked out by the Mother Lode, the Comstock Lode, and the northern mines.

Alemany first sent missionaries to take up residence in the larger mining centers, regarded as key points, from which the priests journeyed to outlying camps and isolated residences. In the field they found that prospectors were often grouped by national origin. For example, the Mexicans named their camp Sonora after the area in Mexico from which most of them came; the Chileans were at Chili Bar; the Chinese, in Chinese Camps. Ethnic groups were mixed in other places such as Bodie which, at its height, drew its population from more than forty countries.

After setting up a residence, the missionary would proceed to hold services and say Mass wherever he could find a public hall or an appropriate private house. After the services, he would hold a meeting to persuade the congregation to build a church and establish an adjoining graveyard. Though this technique was largely successful, few of the early wooden churches are still standing owing to the fires which periodically raged through the flimsy camps.

After churches were built in the mining camps under his charge, the missionary would visit them on a regular basis, according to Walsh, "kindling a fire, sweeping out a hall, hearing confessions, saying Mass, preaching a sermon, (and) teaching catechism." In addition he would perform baptisms and marriages and was on call to come to the dying. Many reminiscences exist of the long journey by horseback taken by priests to administer the last rites of the Church. In some of the larger centers, nuns came to establish Catholic schools. Elsewhere, school was conducted by the priest himself. Fairs and bazaars were held to support the financial needs of the tiny churches, and Catholic children marched prominently in the 4th of July parades. A high point came with the rare and important visit of the bishop to confirm the classes carefully instructed and prepared by the priest.

The predominantly Irish missionaries were augmented by priests sent to particular language groups. For example, Father Edward Sánchez preached in Spanish to the Mexicans, while other priests gathered the French, German, and Slavonic Catholics. One in particular, Father Chan, was sent by Alemany to minister to the Chinese, who often lived in isolation, adjacent to many camps. Many years later, a woman raised in the pioneer mining community of Jamestown, three miles from Sonora, recalled the effect Chan had on her father when he, not the usual priest, came to hold services in 1864.

He was clothed in the customary clerical garb, it was true, but his face was the face of what the Irish used to call a heathen Chinee. [My father] turned on his heel. . . . It was only when he was persuaded to go into the church, and saw the strange creature offer up Mass like any other Catholic clergyman, that he began to believe it. . . . It took all the eloquence of Father Augez himself to persuade the puzzled son of Erin that there were many such priests of the Church in missionary countries, and that this was a Chinese missionary, who had come to Tuolumne County at the request of Archbishop Alemany to evangelize his fellow countrymen at the adjoining town of Chinese Camp.

Walsh notes that Father Chan left Sonora in 1865 "after futile efforts to impress the Chinese miners with truths of Christianity." After a similar lack of success in San Francisco, he moved on to take charge of a Chinese missionary college in Rome.

Though heavy immigration from Italy did not occur until after 1870, parish records in the mining country show that some Italians found their way into the area during the Gold Rush period. After they were forced out by Americans, they returned to San Francisco to settle with Frenchmen, Basques, Mexicans, and Spaniards in an area called the Latin Quarter near Telegraph Hill.

Approximately four Italian men arrived for every immigrating Italian woman. Many of the men hoped to earn enough wealth to return and buy land in Italy where they had left their wives and children. Coming from a country with extreme poverty and profound regional differences, immigration in California came mainly from the northern provinces of Genoa and Lucca on the northwest coast, from Cosenza at the tip of the Italian peninsula and from Palermo in Sicily. It is estimated there were 1,000 Italians in San Francisco by 1860, and 3,000 in the state, nearly a third of the 10,000 that the 1860 census indicated had made their way from Italy to the United States.

The development of a Catholic hierarchy to respond to the increasing (and increasingly heterogeneous) immigration was rapid. The first jurisdictional change had been to remove the peninsula of Baja California, which was still part of Mexico. Then, on July 29, 1853, the Diocese of Monterey was divided along a line just north of Monterey, and Alemany elevated to Archbishop of the new province established at San Francisco. Father Thaddeus Amat, who had previously served in Louisiana, Missouri, and Pennsylvania, was appointed bishop of the southern, less populous Diocese of Monterey which, in 1859, was renamed the Diocese of Monterey-Los Angeles.

Amat arrived in 1855 and found fewer than twenty priests serving his diocese. He first set up his headquarters in Santa Barbara but later moved to Los Angeles. There, in 1856, Father Edmond Venisse described his arrival as follows. "While the ringing of the bells filled the air, the Indians, dressed in their most gorgeous costumes, mingled with ranchers who had come from distant parts." Venisse observed that the crowds in the street formed a "joyous throng" and that "at the approach of the bishop all knelt with respect to receive his blessing." Amat obtained several clerical students from Europe whom he ordained. The Sisters of Charity opened a school and an orphanage in 1856 and, two years later, a hospital. These institutions were joined, in 1865, by St. Vincent's College, opened by the Vincentian Fathers, that, after forty-six years, became Loyola University.

Immigration into the southern Diocese continued to be slow, and its six counties stretching from San Luis Obispo south to the Mexican border continued to be known as the "cow counties" because cattle raising dominated their economy until disastrous droughts destroyed the herds. In 1859 the citizens of these counties voted to be politically detached from Northern California and attached to the more Hispanic and Catholic New Mexico Territory with which they felt a greater affinity; however, the Federal government denied the request. Nonetheless, differences between Northern and Southern California linger on.

A most important development early in Amat's administration was the decision by the United States Land Commission to return title to the Church of the mission buildings and certain of their adjacent properties, action which Alemany had earlier requested. Since sixteen of the twenty-one missions were in Amat's jurisdiction, work to repair and rebuild them became an important part of his responsibility. As Catholics once more worshiped in their thick-walled adobe structures, schools, hospitals, and orphanages were soon built in their vicinity.

While Los Angeles continued to retain its distinctively Spanish flavor and remained essentially Spanish-speaking, San Francisco became increasingly cosmopolitan. By 1860 both French and German congregations had been established in the northern archdiocese. Italian, Spanish, and Portuguese immigrants worshiped at St. Francis's church where they were served by a Chinese priest. Between 1870 and 1880, 15,000 Chinese arrived in San Francisco, and by the end of the decade a successful Catholic mission had been established to serve them.

Italian immigrants continued to take up residence in an area known as Little Italy, which expanded toward Telegraph Hill and North Beach, and in a second area around Mission Dolores. San Francisco became unique among American cities in that northerners and southerners from Italy settled together in substantial numbers. However their social relations remained structured by regional mutual aid societies, each of which kept the statue of a patron saint in its meeting hall.

Internal struggles on the Italian peninsula in the nineteenth century, struggles which pitted impoverished peasants against the land-owning Church, had made many Italian men ambivalent about Catholicism as an institution with loyalties much more closely grounded in the family. Indeed, few immigrant men had attended church in Italy. Far more important to them was the yearly procession of the regional society with the statue of their saint at its head. Within San Francisco's Little Italy these sentiments could still be found. When the Pope ceded Rome to the unified Italian state in 1871, there were those who rejoiced.

It was the Irish Catholic missionaries who found the most compatriots in residence. In 1858, Largan from All Hallows had estimated that of those walking the streets in San Francisco, "one-third of the population is Irish, though many try to deny it." From the end of the Civil War to 1870, 20,000 Irish settled in San Francisco and by 1880, they totaled 30,000 and were the largest foreign group in the city.

Rather than settling in a single area, the Irish immigrants spread evenly throughout the city. Their experience differed markedly from that of the Irish on the East Coast where they grouped themselves tightly in cities which had Protestant power structures going back two hundred years. As with the Italians, four Irish men arrived for every woman. This difference, combined with the atmosphere of freedom and pluralism, led to many mixed marriages. One result was *A Treatise on Matrimony* (1864) written by Amat and a letter from Alemany and his bishops to the Catholics of the Province of San Francisco eight years later. Amat referred to mixed marriage as "nothing else but a palliated concubinage" and Alemany called it a practice which "the Church abhors." The impact of these judgments is difficult to assess. However, attitudes toward birth control in California may be inferred from the census of 1870, which shows that in San Francisco the Irish, with only 2.3 children per family, were producing far smaller families than was typical of Catholics elsewhere in the country.

In California the Irish rose rapidly in politics and financial eminence and, with their presence in large numbers in the clergy, dominated the Church which provided them with community centers. Devotional societies began to develop, with the first, dedicated to the Blessed Virgin Mary, organized in 1861. However, Irish hegemony had its limits. When the clergy railed against "devotions of pagan Mediterraneans" and tried to persuade the Italians to bring the statues of their saints from their meeting halls to the churches, they were largely unsuccessful. It wasn't until the Salesian Fathers arrived to assist in 1897 that they had any real success with the Italians, but by then the importance of the saints and processions in promoting regional loyalties was beginning to fade.

As the population in the hinterlands grew, the Vicariate-Apostolic of Marysville, which contained many of the mining camps served by Catholic missionaries, was detached from the Archdiocese of San Francisco and enlarged to include a portion of the new state of Nevada. When established, in 1860, it had a Catholic population within California of approximately 30,000. Eight years later it became the Diocese of Grass Valley under Bishop Eugene O'Connell. O'Connell, a distinguished theologian from All Hallows, had been loaned to Alemany in 1851 and was first sent to head the Diocesan seminary in Santa Ynez. When it failed to thrive, O'Connell was brought back to San Francisco to be pastor at Mission Dolores. While there, he established St. Mary's as the Diocesan seminary. After his three-year service in California, O'Connell returned to Ireland to become Dean of All Hallows College, until he was recalled to California in 1860 to supervise the newly emerging diocese in the gold country.

In 1869 a transcontinental railroad joined San Francisco to the Eastern states, and the first of the rail cars passed the last of the Conestoga wagons bringing immigrants to California. By 1870 the population of San Francisco was 149,473 compared to the 5,728 in still Spanish-speaking Los Angeles.

The railroad, however, did not arrive in time to transport California's three bishops on the first leg of their trip to the First Vatican Council in Rome. Traveling by steamship down the coast of Baja California and across the Isthmus of Panama by rail, Alemany, Amat, and O'Connell joined with bishops summoned by the Pope from around the world. Called by Pope Pius IX to foster confidence in the doctrinal authority of the Church at a time when it was losing temporal power, the most important issue discussed was that of papal infallibility.

The three California bishops did not agree on whether or how "papal infallibility" should be defined. Amat, along with nearly half of the American prelates, was among those opposed to the definition. However, in the final session he assented and the three California bishops kissed the Pope's ring just as the armies of a united Italy marched into Rome to strip the papacy of its temporal power and to leave it essentially imprisoned in the Vatican until the Concordat of 1929.

Amat became ill shortly after his return from Rome and, at his request, Francis Mora, a Catalonian who had accompanied him in 1855, was appointed coadjutor in 1873. On Amat's death in 1878, Mora was appointed Bishop of the Diocese of Monterey-Los Angeles and he saw the beginnings of the first large population shift in Southern California. In 1880, of the 864,694 people in California, it was estimated that 219,000 were Catholics. Of these, 185,000 were in the Archdiocese of San Francisco, 24,000 were in the Diocese of Monterey-Los Angeles; and 10,000 remained in the California portion of the Diocese of Grass Valley, which had lost numbers as the mining districts had declined.

The population of Los Angeles in 1880 was 11,183 which, though small, was double that of 1870. However, with the arrival of the Santa Fe Railroad in the early 1880s, the land boom in Southern California was on. Mora continued to build Catholic churches and by 1890 there were five with a concurrent development of Catholic schools.

With massive immigration from the midwest, the character of Los Angeles changed from that of a Spanish town to that of a midwestern, Protestant-dominated city. By the turn of the century, the population of Los Angeles had grown to 102,479 of which only one-fifth was estimated to be Catholic. One of the important challenges to Bishop George Montgomery (who succeeded Mora) was the protection of Catholics from the newly organized American Protective Association, a midwestern nativist association whose members pledged never to vote for, hire, or strike with a Catholic.

While the population of Los Angeles grew, some of the northeastern counties of the state declined. As the Diocese of Grass Valley lost Catholics when miners moved on and once booming camps became ghost-towns, it was reorganized in 1886 with the addition of ten counties and renamed the Diocese of Sacramento. O'Connell had earlier requested a coadjutor bishop and received Patrick Manogue, who was appointed his successor in 1884 and became the first bishop of the reorganized diocese.

As a young man Manogue had participated in the Gold Rush and found enough gold to finance his seminary education at the Sulpician Academy in Paris. He returned to a parish on the Comstock Lode in Nevada, which covered an immense territory of sagebrush. Here he converted the Native Americans as well as ministered to the miners whose cares he understood because he had been one himself. Walsh tells how he once rode 180 miles to prepare for death a man who had been sentenced to hang. Finding extenuating circumstances, he returned 180 miles through a blizzard to obtain a reprieve and finally a full pardon from the governor of the territory.

One of Manogue's first projects as bishop was to build the Cathedral of the Most Blessed Sacrament in Sacramento. In 1895, Manogue was succeeded by Bishop Thomas Grace who, after preparing at All Hallows College and Dublin Missionary School, served as a priest in the mining towns for twenty-nine years.

Meanwhile, in San Francisco, Alemany retired in 1884 and returned to Spain. The press reported that as his train passed, "three hundred people . . . instinctively fell upon their knees to receive his blessing" and called it "a graceful and beautiful homage to a man whose religious devotion is so thoroughly apostolic." Patrick J. Riordan was appointed archbishop to succeed him. He had served as Alemany's coadjutor and was prepared to start immediately on what contemporaries termed an "exceptionally active era of parish church building."

San Francisco continued to develop as a cosmopolitan city. With an increase in German immigration, the 60,000 Germans in the city at the turn of the century almost equaled the 70,000 Irish. The Italians remained the third largest ethnic group. Because of restrictive immigration laws, the Chinese population, which had reached a peak of 26,000 in 1890, had shrunk to 15,000 by 1900.

As the twentieth century dawned, in a total population in California of 1,485,053, there were 308,000 Catholics worshiping in eighty-three parish churches in the Archdiocese of San Francisco, in forty-three parish churches in Monterey-Los Angeles, and in thirty-three parish churches in the California portion of the Diocese of Sacramento. In addition, there were numerous hospitals, welfare institutions, parish schools, high schools, academies, missions, three colleges and four seminaries. What was said by a contemporary of the work of the Catholic Church in San Francisco could be said of the entire state: It was "as broad and deep as life itself. From the cradle to the grave all are taken care of."

The Catholic Church in California had become an integral part of the Catholic Church in America. When in January of 1899 the papal encyclical, *Testem Benevolentiae*, was issued, which called the orthodoxy of the Roman Catholic Church in America into question, its concluding summation was closely studied throughout the Golden State, particularly the suggestion that there may be "some among you who conceive of and desire a church in America different from that which is in the rest of the world."

Already there were Catholics who realized their church had

origins in California which differed from the manner in which it had come into being elsewhere. Built in a period of unparalleled population growth over the course of half a century, unhindered by preceding Protestant power structures, shaped in an atmosphere of extreme ethnic pluralism, and comfortable with the complete separation of church and state, Californian Catholicism had developed historically in a new way. With its experience of freedom, its sensitivity to religious pluralism, and its willingness to broadly participate with other Christian groups, it was already different from the Catholic Church in many other parts of the world.

Its pioneering period past, the Catholic Church in California was poised and ready to welcome the immigrants and refugees from many lands, the latest of those who saw in California a land of opportunity. In the twentieth century Southern California became the crucible for the blending of the Catholicism of previously disparate groups and the agent for the development of an Hispanic Catholicism of a new type in America.

FURTHER READING:
Dolan, Jay P. *The American Catholic Experience.* New York: Doubleday, 1985.
Ellis, John Tracy. *American Catholicism.* Chicago: The University of Chicago Press, 1956.
Hennesey, James, S.J., *American Catholics: A History of the Roman Catholic Community in the United States.* Oxford: Oxford University Press, 1981.
Walsh, Henry., S.J. *Hallowed Were the Gold Dust Trails.* Santa Clara, California: University of Santa Clara Press, 1946.
Weber, Francis J. *Documents of California Catholic History.* Los Angeles: Dawson's Book Store, 1965.

3 Hispanic Crucible

The missions built in California are our title deeds to show the newcomers that we of the Old Church are in California by the right of inheritance.
　　—John Joseph Cantwell, Archbishop of Los Angeles, 1941

The nineteenth century has been termed the immigrant century for the Catholic Church in the United States. And so it was for European Catholic immigrants who either clustered in East Coast cities dominated by established Protestant groups or pioneered in the northern Midwest. However, the experience of many Catholics in California during this period was very different. Nineteenth century California included many descendants of the original Spanish Catholic power elite who intermixed with the Sonoran settlers from northern Mexico as well as with the native population. These *Californios* fought—unsuccessfully—to maintain their cattle-raising culture against inrushing European immigrants after the Gold Rush.

After the secularization of the missions in 1834, the number of Mexican land grants in California grew from less than 100 to over 1,000. With statehood came many disputes over the legal status of title to property, and the United States Congress, in 1851, created a

Land Commission to settle competing land claims. The Commission, based in San Francisco, examined more than 800 land grants of which eventually 604 were found to be valid. The *Californios*, especially those with great ranches in Southern California, were at a particular disadvantage as the Land Commission was far to the north, none of the commissioners spoke Spanish, and the *rancheros* were unfamiliar with Anglo-Saxon law.

In spite of these disadvantages, some *Californios* managed to save their ranches and, in the waning years of the nineteenth century, continued their cattle-raising, *vaquero* culture romanticized by writers such as Helen Hunt Jackson and Charles Lummis. It is this group that nourished Hispanic Catholicism in California, a group that, when combined with Hispanic Catholics living elsewhere in the Southwest, laid the foundation for a type of Catholicism that now represents one-third of the Catholics in the United States.

Hispanic Catholicism is a complex phenomenon weaving together the experiences of individuals with, except for their Spanish Catholic heritage, very different backgrounds. The Mexican communities in Santa Barbara, San Diego, and Los Angeles were the surviving cultural core for this kind of Catholicism in Southern California.

The pueblo of Los Angeles had first been settled in 1781 by Sonorans of a mixed Spanish, Native American, and African extraction. By 1836, approximately 2,200 Mexicans were spread throughout the city. As Anglo immigrants arrived in Los Angeles after statehood, the Mexican-Americans (along with the Chinese) began to congregate in an area of the city known as Sonora Town. When St. Vibiana's Cathedral was built in 1876, they remained loyal to the Catholic Church on the plaza, nicknamed "La Placita," which came to symbolize the center of Hispanic Catholicism for Los Angeles. Gradually as the Anglo-American population overwhelmed them, they moved into the poorer areas of the city to congregate in *barrios*. By 1930 the barrios east of the Los Angeles River had grown together to become the largest Mexican-American barrio in the United States. Eventually, Los Angeles had the largest population of Mexican origin of any city, with the exception of Mexico City.

Immigrants to California from the New Mexico territory brought with them a different form of Catholicism. This territory achieved statehood in 1912 when Arizona and New Mexico were admitted to the Union, but the early settlers and native populations of the area had created a shared culture that was maintained well into the twentieth century. This southwestern culture included an indigenous form of Catholicism built up over three centuries of Spanish occupation of native lands. Aspects of it are still evident in New Mexico in the form of stark but beautiful white-washed adobe churches often located in Native American pueblos as well as in the windowless, wooden meeting houses of the penitentials. Borrowing from the penitential practices of the Franciscans, who had been the first missionaries into the area, southwestern Catholicism also draws heavily on local practices, particularly those concerning healing. Catholicism in California reflects these influences as well.

Gradually in the mid-nineteenth century, under the direction of the archbishops of California and New Mexico, a more European form of Catholicism was introduced. However, this form became dominant only in widely scattered urban centers where parochial schools were also established. Rural practices, in many places, were left relatively untouched. Therefore, to understand the non-European Catholic influence in California, it is necessary to picture it first against a background of vast stretches of desert, as a rural rather than urban phenomenon, which was more typical of Catholic experience elsewhere in America. When it did move into cities, this southwestern Catholicism tended to become located in barrios, such as the one in East Los Angeles—a tightly compacted area, where Spanish is still spoken and a vibrant Hispanic culture generally is still maintained.

In addition to the southwestern and *Californio* types of Catholicism in California, yet another contribution to Hispanic Catholicism was introduced into California by Native American immigrants to the state. In the late nineteenth century, reservations were established for Native American groups, predominantly in the present states of Arizona, New Mexico, and Texas, and Catholic churches appeared in them as missionary enterprises. Later, some Native

Americans moved off their reservations into local towns and cities, many in California. They brought their own forms of native and Catholic practices with them, contributing to developing Hispanic Catholicism in California more significantly than California's own indigenous native populations, many of whom had intermarried and become culturally absorbed or, if they had remained culturally distinct, had survived only as scattered remnants.

These groups were joined after the Spanish American War by yet another group of Catholic immigrants from the Philippines who completed the Hispanic base for the groundswell of immigrants who began to arrive from predominantly Central and Southern Mexico after the Mexican Revolution of 1910. These newest arrivals settled in urban areas or worked on farms as *braceros* (farm laborers who work with their arms). They brought to California a type of Mexican culture different from that of the earlier Sonorans, one more reminiscent of the profusion of flowers and colorful fiestas of their native land. It was this type of Mexican Catholic culture, found familiar by later Central American immigrants, that came to dominate Californian Hispanic Catholicism.

Some Mexican-American Catholics appear only nominally Catholic, exhibiting an aloofness to the Church that sometimes is viewed as echoing the anti-clericalism of their homeland. An alternative understanding, however, is found in seeing how profoundly Mexican Catholicism is a "folk religion." In fact, as John M. Ingham demonstrates, folk Catholicism—a blend of pre-Columbian religion with Spanish Catholicism—permeates Mexican culture, expressing "to an extraordinary degree" rather than contradicting the Catholic worldview. In an ethno-historical study of the Nahua community of Tlayacapan in the highlands of Morelos south of Mexico city, Ingham provides a detailed picture of the kind of folk Catholicism imported into California beginning in 1910. It is unmistakably Catholic, but exhibits an independence from the Church that gives an appearance of aloofness.

At the time of the Conquest, the Spanish found a culture in Central Mexico based on the clan that included both nobles and commoners. Each clan had its own deity with the nobles and chiefs responsible for preparing the festivals in its honor. After the Spanish Conquest, this pattern of social organization was adapted to the cult of the saints located in local chapels and shrines, a part of lay religiosity in Christendom since the eleventh century. The saints offer protection, particularly for crops; and chapels where miraculous occurrences have taken place become shrines and pilgrimage centers visited by neighboring villagers. It is estimated that in Mexico about one village in six has such a shrine. In California, these pre-Columbian roots persist in respect for the person of the *aya-munto* (mayor) and in the prevalence of house shrines which duplicate those found in Mexico.

Godparenting is an important social, cultural and religious institution in Mexican folk religion. Sacramental godparents are chosen to oversee and contribute to the festivities surrounding baptism, confirmation, First Communion, and marriage. Two sets of relationships are established: *padrinazgo*, which links godparents to a godchild, and *compadrazgo*, which links godparents to the child's parents. In Tlayacapán, as different godparents are usually chosen for each of the sacramental occasions, and as further linkages occur through marriage, godparenting provides a complex system reflecting community goals of moral development and mutual respect.

The responsibilities taken on by godparents are evident in the *quince años*, which combines the celebration of a girl's fifteenth birthday, her saint's day, and the commemoration of her baptism. It provides a particularly important role for an individual who has been a godfather for fifteen years. Ingham describes how, following a mass at the church, the celebration ideally involves a feast and dancing at the parents' house. The girl wears an elegant red dress and high heels, and she is accompanied by fifteen *damas* (maids) in red or blue dresses and a *chambelan* (escort) in a dark suit. As her choice, the escort is understood to be possibly her future fiancé. The young woman dances first with her godfather, then with her father, and then with the chambelan. The godfather, on this occasion, is responsible for taking the girl aside to explain about men and how she, as a grown woman, should now comport herself. In California this celebration has often been extravagantly adapted, with the young woman in a white prom dress, the young man in black dinner clothes, and the feast in a hotel. Though often deplored by the clergy as unbearably expensive for many families, the celebration retains its popularity.

Godparents are also chosen for occasions of special blessings not considered sacramental but which, according to Ingham, "are thought to provide remission from venial sin and freedom from the power of evil spirits." On these occasions godparents function in a manner analogous to their role in sacraments. For example the rite of *evangélios*—to treat fright possibly brought about by meeting a ghost—involves readings by a priest from the Gospels, sprinkling with holy water, touching, and a benediction. On this occasion, godparents with particularly "strong blood," such as virile adolescents, are sought who also touch the patient after the priest.

Immigrants moving north brought other religious traditions with them. Perhaps the most ubiquitous is devotion to the Virgin of Guadalupe, whose shrine outside of Mexico City is located on the Hill of Tepeyec, sacred in pre-Conquest times to the goddess Tonantzín. Her image is reproduced countless times in California in house shrines as well as in Catholic churches. When César Chavez organized the United Farm Workers in California in 1966 to fight for better wages and working conditions for migrant Mexican laborers, he placed the Virgin of Guadalupe on his banner just as had the insurgents in the Mexican war of independence.

If the Virgin of Guadalupe represents the ideal of the chaste and interceding mother, other images convey the opposite kind of woman. *La Llarona*, it is told, wanders at night calling for her aborted children. She appears in flowing white veils with unkempt hair, a seductive figure luring men who, when they remove her veil, see a horse's face. She resembles the pre-Hispanic goddess Cihuacoatl, or Tonantzín, who caused adversity, poverty, and discouragement. La Llarona is still remembered in California. When a young Californian recently asked his great-grandmother to tell him about what she remembered of the religion of her native land, she told him the following.

Long ago in Mexico lived a woman. In that time they had no birth control. This woman wandered at night and had many boy friends. When she would become pregnant, she would always try to hide it. When she gave birth she drowned her babies in the river. When she died God did not accept her soul. God sent her back to find her children. To this day, if you listen late at night, you can hear her crying wherever running water is found, searching and crying for her lost children.

The male counterpart of La Llarona is the Devil, who may appear on horseback in a well tailored *charro* suit with tight pants, his eyes like burning coals. His agents, called *pingos*, also appear on horseback and all are reminiscent of the wealthy Spanish or creole *hacendados* (ranch owners). Ingham points out that though evil assumes various manifestations, "the essence that evil beings would appropriate is variously the soul, a person's virility or fecundity, or his or her labor." In this sense, evil beings are the opposite of God and the saints who strengthen the soul and give support to economic production as well as to biological and cultural reproduction.

Evil supernatural beings have their counterpart in witches (called *brujos*) who, having made pacts with the devil, are able to make people sick or poor. Though elusive, witchcraft is much talked about throughout much of the southwestern United States and Mexico, and has been brought into California. Seeing themselves as well meaning folk curers, practitioners of witchcraft are often simply persons who are believed by their neighbors to know how to cure *susto* (fright) or ward off the evil eye.

Particular celebrations of the liturgical calendar also came north with the new immigrants. For example, a ceremonial cycle celebrated both in Mexico and California begins with Advent marked by both the *fiesta* of the Immaculate Conception on December 8 and that of the Virgin of Guadalupe on December 12. Beginning on December 16, nativity scenes are set up in homes and celebrations of *Las Posadas* (the Inns) are held for the nine nights before Christmas. Processions with children dressed as Mary, Joseph, the Angel, and the shepherds may go from door to door seeking lodging or, in simpler versions, carolers may simply sing Mexican songs such as *"Las Mananitas,"* the birthday song. The evening's festivities may close with the breaking of a *piñata*, a large *papier mâché* container in some form, such as an animal, decorated with crêpe paper and filled with candies. These ceremonies differ from the traditional Shepherd's Play, with its struggle between good and evil for the soul, which was widely celebrated in the early California missions and is still performed in the reconstructed chapel of the Presidio in Santa Barbara.

The liturgical cycle, which includes the observance of Lent (the forty days before Easter), special services during Holy Week (at the end of Lent), and Pentecost (celebrated on the seventh Sunday after Easter), ends with the celebration of All Saints' Day and All Souls' Day on November 1 and 2. On the former, dead baptized children who as innocents have gone straight to heaven are remembered, while on the latter, food offerings are taken to cemeteries where they are shared with neighbors and with the adult dead in purgatory. In Tlayacapán, persons are understood to have a spirit received from God with the "breath of life," a second shadow soul located in the bloodstream, and a third night-air soul having a malevolent quality, which may appear clothed in the shadow soul as a ghost. This tripartite view is consistent with the Platonic and neo-Platonic roots of the Church but not with the judgment of the ninth-century church council, nor with Thomistic theology which understands the spirit and soul to be one. The spirit may also be considered to be a guardian angel that looks after the soul which suffers for sins after death. Funeral rites are concerned with seeing that the shadow soul is appeased and that it and the body are properly buried.

Ingham concludes that rather than viewing the acceptance of Christian belief and practices by the Mexican native populations as superficial, the missionary friars found substantial parallels between the store of Christian customs transmitted to Mexico in the sixteenth century and the pre-Hispanic religion. Therefore, "the result of conversion was a folk Catholicism that was at once more Catholic and more pagan than the lay religion found elsewhere in Catholic countrysides." Importantly, he finds the root metaphor—the basic concept that informs an entire worldview of this Mexican folk Catholicism—to be "reproduction."

A brief review of relations between the government of the

Republic of Mexico and the Catholic Church in the nineteenth and twentieth centuries is also relevant for understanding Hispanic Catholicism in California. After the war of independence, which lasted from 1810 to 1821, there was a struggle over the *Patronato* with the Church declaring the state did not inherit the rights enjoyed by the Spanish kings.

A federal type of constitution, modeled on that of the United States, was adopted in 1824, with an important exception. Instead of forbidding the establishment of any religion, as does the first amendment of the Bill of Rights to the United States Constitution, Article II of the Mexican constitution states, "The religion of the Mexican nation is and will be perpetually the Roman Catholic Apostolic. The nation will protect it by wise and just laws and will prohibit the exercise of any other."

In spite of this constitution, the church and the state continued to struggle. Laws of reform promulgated in 1859 and, absorbed into subsequent constitutions, not only eliminated the clergy from public office but curtailed its members' right to vote. All the wealth in the hands of regular and secular clergy was confiscated and the acquisition of further wealth, even by gift, was forbidden in the future. Church and state were separated, freedom of religion was proclaimed, and all regular orders along with their confraternities were abolished. Their churches were turned over to the hierarchy and their possessions, except for vessels and vestments, became the property of the government. Civil marriage was established and civil justices put in charge of marriage registries and cemeteries.

Further restrictions followed, culminating in the expulsion of the religious orders and the founding of the lay apostolate orders of *Las Sociedades Católicas de Señores y Señoras*. Members of these groups assisted priests in catechizing children preparing for their First Communion a quarter of a century before Pope Pius X, in 1905, directed that such programs should be established in every parish and half a century before Bishop John J. Cantwell of Los Angeles directed the major development of the Confraternity of Christian Doctrine (CCD) in Los Angeles.

Proferio Díaz, president of Mexico from 1877 to 1911, followed a policy of conciliation of the Church by permitting the reestablishment of religious communities, never attacking worship in the churches, and permitting Catholic schools. During this period, the numbers of parishes, seminaries, seminarians, and religious orders all increased. Even though the reform laws limited public worship to the interior of buildings, enthusiasm for public feasts and processions caused the laws to be frequently broken.

The Revolution of 1910, led by Francisco Y. Madero and others, overthrew Díaz and sent him into exile. The turmoil in Mexico which accompanied the revolution initiated the flight of refugees across the northern border. In Los Angeles they mostly settled in the Plaza area and existing barrios where they compounded problems of already congested housing. It was estimated that four out of every five families of Mexican origin were living in houses without baths at this time. In 1914, though this group represented 5 percent of the population of Los Angeles, they accounted for 11.1 percent of the deaths.

When Bishop John J. Cantwell was installed as head of the Diocese of Monterey–Los Angeles in 1917, one of his first acts was to organize an immigrant welfare bureau within the Associated Catholic Charities. A settlement house with a free medical clinic was established. It was useful that such a clinic had already been established when, in 1924 and 1925, some 140,000 rats invaded Sonora Town with a subsequent outbreak of bubonic plague, in which five people died.

Francis J. Weber judges that the Confraternity of Christian Doctrine, brought to Los Angeles in 1923, was "probably the single most effective of the many programs" designed for the immigrants. In thirteen years it had in operation 211 centers with 1,279 teachers instructing 28,500 students and was being widely copied elsewhere in the United States.

Plutarco Calles became president of Mexico in 1924 and began a violent anti-clerical campaign. The bishops in Mexico responded by closing all the churches for a period of three years. Peasant Catholics launched the merciless *Cristero* rebellion in 1927, during which Los Angeles served as a major support base. It has been suggested that Edward Doheny, a papal count, builder of St. John's seminary, and richest Catholic in Los Angeles, provided part of this support. Doheny, along with his partner Harry Sinclair, had wildcatted in the Tampico oil fields, and they remained the biggest foreign investors in Mexico.

At the close of the revolt in 1929, a short-lived measure of peace between the president of Mexico and the Mexican church hierarchy was restored, which made possible the return of most of the clergy and members of the religious orders to Mexico. This caused an added problem because few of the priests born in the United States could speak the tongue of the refugees who decided to remain. Seminarians were encouraged to study Spanish and the Mexican culture, and provisions were made for them to spend time in Mexico in order to prepare for work among the Mexicans and Mexican-Americans, mainly present in the Southwest and California, as well as the continuing stream of immigrants.

The rapid growth of the Diocese of Monterey-Los Angeles brought jurisdictional changes. In 1922, the Diocese of Monterey-Fresno was made a separate diocese, and the remaining territory was renamed the Diocese of Los Angeles-San Diego.

In 1936, partially in recognition of the fact that Los Angeles was outpacing San Francisco as the population center of the state, Pope Pius XI established Los Angeles as a metropolitan district, making California the only state in the union to have two archbishops. At the same time, San Diego was made a separate diocese.

While great changes were being made at the hierarchical level, the building of parishes continued. A son tells what his mother remembers of these years.

My mother was born in East Los Angeles in 1937 and her family moved into a neighborhood in an industrial section of East Los Angeles in 1941 near the Southern Pacific Tracks. The parish they belonged to was Resurrection Church which was about six miles away. The family seldom attended Mass until an old garage and gas station were converted into a satellite chapel of the main parish about five blocks from their home.

When my mother was in first grade, two nuns were assigned to teach catechism to about twenty children from the local grammar school. The classes were held in the chapel. The nuns were so graceful, gentle and caring that they became key figures in my mother's young life. The catechism classes grew larger each week and many surrounding neighbors offered their garages and back yards to accommodate the many new classes.

If anyone wished to attend Bible classes, festivals or other church functions, they had to go to Resurrection Church. Not many people seemed interested in going out of their neighborhood. My mother does remember the nuns starting a club for girls called Sodality. The club met every two weeks. They made crafts and did charitable deeds for parishioners in need. They also started a small library of children's religious books for students to check out.

As more immigrants moved into the area, the numbers of families attending Mass at the chapel increased and more Masses were added. At about this time, it was decided that the chapel should have its own name and it was dedicated as "Our Lady of Victory," perhaps because of the victory at the end of World War II. Through the years the Chapel became a focal point in the lives of all the surrounding community since most of the population was Catholic in the area. A typical week in the church was Mass on Sundays, catechism classes on Mondays and Wednesdays, and Sodality every other Thursday. Confessions were heard on Saturday.

This was a period of unprecedented growth for Southern California. Between 1937 and 1947 the number of Catholics in the Archdiocese of Los Angeles doubled from 300,000 to 601,200 with the majority of that growth owing to Hispanic immigration. This rate of growth outpaced that of the nation, which took twenty years, between 1940 and 1960, for Catholic membership to double from 21 to 42 million.

Archbishop J. Francis A. McIntyre, who arrived in Los Angeles in 1948, addressed growth in Southern California with an accelerated program of building. Between 1948 and 1963, eighty-two parishes were founded; Catholic schools trebled from 141 to 347; eight seminaries, six general hospitals, and forty-nine new religious communities were added. Catholics continued to flow into the Archdiocese at the rate of 1,000 a week.

Since the beginning of the twentieth century, the Catholics in California had become increasingly integrated into the American Catholic Church and participated in its trends. After World War II, Catholic veterans used the G.I. Bill to attend secular colleges and universities in unprecedented numbers. At the same time, Catholic colleges in California, as elsewhere in the nation, required their students to take courses in traditional Catholic philosophy and theology which resulted, according to the Catholic historian John Cogley, in the "most theologically sophisticated generation of laymen in the history of the Church." These groups of lay men and women, rising in prosperity, moved to the suburbs to raise families.

The new generation of well-educated Catholics read the works of European Catholic theologians and were aware of efforts to bring the Catholic Church into the modern world by reconciling it with science and historical/critical methods of studying biblical texts. Closer to home they were also likely to be aware of the liturgical reforms being urged by Benedictine monks. And though they were apt to remain concerned about what William Clebsch described as "living rightly . . . the quest for a clean heart," and to observe the film recommendations of the Legion of Decency emanating from Los Angeles, they were also beginning to develop independent views on questions such as mechanical means of birth control and remarriage. According to a *Catholic Digest* national survey in 1953, only 51 percent of the Catholics surveyed at this time considered these acts to be wrong.

McIntyre was created a cardinal in 1953 and was active in the preliminary planning for the second Vatican Council. The Council, which met in Rome from 1962 to 1965, set into motion a profound series of events that changed the face of the Church. In California the changes were more welcomed than deplored. A survey conducted by *America* magazine in 1966 indicated that the Archdiocese of Los Angeles was "far ahead of other jurisdictions" in implementing the changes mandated by the Council, but these changes brought new problems.

The change from the Latin Mass to Masses in the vernacular

meant many Catholic churches in Southern California needed to schedule at least one Spanish language Mass on Sunday morning in addition to the ones in English. This put added pressure on the bishops in California to find and recruit Spanish-speaking priests. When, in 1967, a century and a half after the dispute was initiated, a settlement was finally reached with Mexico over the Pious Fund: the cash settlement was earmarked for educating Mexicans intending to become priests who were studying in the United States.

Bishops and archbishops attending the second Vatican Council had pressed for a more conciliar form of government to balance the centralized power of the pope and curia. One of the first fruits of the move toward shared authority was a meeting of bishops from throughout the Americas held in Medellín, Colombia, in 1968. An important voice at the conference was that of the Peruvian theologian, Gustavo Gutiérrez, who was reconsidering issues of faith, grace, and truth from the perspective of the poor in Latin America.

The gradual shift to focusing on the poor by the Catholic bishops of Latin America reflects the changing face of Catholicism in a world where the majority of Catholics now live in Third World countries. Penny Lernoux notes that if the Church were given a face, "its color would not be white" because by the end of the century an estimated 70 percent of all Catholics will live in the Third World, "with Latin America counting for the largest number." Los Angeles reflects this face as does the Catholic Church nationally. It is estimated that if present immigration patterns persist, by the year 2000 Hispanics will represent a majority of the Catholics in the United States.

Liberation theology, which developed out of the Medellín conference, addresses these demographic developments by focusing on economic and political liberation and social activism. Catholic activists consider their activities to have been sanctioned by the Vatican II redefinition of the Church as a community of believers, that is as the "people of God" or *pueblo de Diós*. In Latin America, the *pueblo de Diós* is understood to refer to the masses, the crowded poor of the cities, rather than the landed aristocrats. Increasingly the voices of the poor, guided by members of the Catholic religious orders, are heard speaking up in meetings of their small base communities.

In the late sixties, social activism on the part of the Hispanic minorities in Los Angeles was also on the rise. This represented a change from earlier decades when, under the paternalism of Bishop Cantwell, Hispanics had limited their marching to the annual Corpus Christi procession moving from Our Lady of Guadalupe to La Soledad on the East Side.

Little had changed under the even more conservative guidance of Francis McIntyre, appointed archbishop in 1948 and raised to cardinal in 1953. According to the historian, Mike Davis, it was not until after Vatican II that younger clergy "began to question McIntyre's autocracy and to confront his reactionary political position." During this period, an underground church began to develop as contributions to the archdiocese dropped 40 percent. McIntyre fought back by sending undercover priests and monsignors with hidden tape recorders into the homes of underground Catholics. Scores of dissident priests and nuns were removed and, according to Davis, "some exiled to McIntyre's favorite Siberia—Orange County," which was not made a separate diocese until 1976. An Italian Jesuit, visiting Los Angeles in the late sixties, wrote to Rome that "priests in Los Angeles . . . work in an atmosphere of sheer terror."

On Christmas Eve, 1969, one hundred Chicanos of the *Católicos por la Raza*, demanding an equal voice in the archdiocese, marched from Lafayette Park to St. Basil's, where McIntyre was conducting the service. They held a prayer vigil on the steps that was broken up by mass arrests and beatings. Appearing in greater numbers on Christmas Day to form a picket line, they inspired McIntyre to compare them to "the rabble at Christ's crucifixion."

In the face of an increasingly demoralized archdiocese, McIntyre, in his mid-eighties, soon announced his retirement. He was replaced by Timothy Manning in 1970 who, three years later, was made a cardinal. Manning took immediate steps to win back the inner city. He abandoned McIntyre's opulent residence and moved back to St. Vibiana's Cathedral. He also established a consultative priests' senate. Most important, he took steps to reconcile Hispanic Catholics, introducing bilingual classes into parochial schools and nominating Ecuador-born Juan Arzurbe as the first Hispanic (auxiliary) bishop.

These moves came none too soon. Pentecostal Protestant churches with Hispanic ministers and Spanish-language services were making substantial inroads into traditional Hispanic Catholic territory. Surveys conducted in the '70s indicate the conversion of perhaps a fifth of Spanish-surname Catholics in Los Angeles to other religions during the decade, twice the loss nationwide. Evangelicals defended their proselytizing by maintaining that up to 80 percent of Latinos lacked an active relationship with the Church.

Davis suggests "the real issue remained empowerment versus paternalism." In 1948 Manning had spoken of a "Celto-Californian" religious synthesis—a "blend of green and brown, rain and sunshine, a perfect mating of two traditions of faith." Manning's clinging to what Davis refers to as his "personal version of the Mission Myth" prevented him, according to Davis, from dealing with the incongruity of the continuing Celtic leadership over an archdiocese that, by the end of his reign, was nearly 70 percent Hispanic. As an example of his ineptitude, Davis cites the failure of the Vatican, in consultation with Manning, to appoint an Hispanic bishop to the newly established, predominantly Hispanic diocese created in 1978 to encompass Riverside and San Bernardino counties. Two similar opportunities were lost when the diocese of Orange was established in 1976 and that of San Jose in 1981.

However, the irony is that Bishop Philip Straling, the Vatican's choice for the diocese of San Bernardino, took the lead in supporting the organization of Hispanic *comunidades eclesiales de base* in his diocese. According to the *Los Angeles Times*, "Latino activists say the diocese of San Bernardino has become a showplace of base communities—non-territorial parishes governed by lay ministers."

During this period, liberation theology continued to have a substantial impact in California as well as elsewhere in the United States. Juan Arzurbe was instrumental in bringing it to Los Angeles. He supported small, intense evangelical study groups on the east side, as well as Spanish-speaking prayer communities. These served as a base for the United Neighborhood Organization (UNO) which began to train grass-roots political leaders.

Though liberation theology has been understood as a specific response to the complex problems of a particular area, it was certainly not irrelevant to the two pastoral letters issued by the U.S. bishops on nuclear war and economics in the past decade. The method the bishops pursued—distributing copies of early drafts for comment—resembles the practice of Latin American bishops who circulated important documents to base communities for discussion.

When the American bishops issued the final version of their pastoral letter on economics in 1986, it directly addressed issues that were rapidly becoming compelling in California. Between 1980 and 1990, the population of the state grew from 24 million to 30 million with most of the growth due to immigration from Latin America and Asia. As a politician of this period put it, California, the major recipient of the failed U.S. foreign policy, had become the new Ellis Island of America. Housing became unaffordable, schools overcrowded with non-English speakers, and the freeways jammed. The new immigrants had to choose between moving in with earlier arrivals, living in their cars, or living on the streets.

In this situation, the gulf visibly widened between the Californians who are members of the privileged 0.5 percent of U.S. households possessing 35 percent of the nation's wealth, and those numbered among the 98 percent holding 46 percent of the country's net financial assets. By stating that economic rights are part of fundamental human rights and that a preferential option must be given to the poor, the American bishops directly addressed the needs of the Hispanic and Asian immigrants in California.

During this period, repercussions of events in Latin America swept over the Hispanic communities in the United States. As immigrants continued to come north from every point in Central and South America, they established small ethnic communities usually organized around their common Catholic heritage but also organized outside the Church. For example, a group of immigrating Argentineans in Los Angeles gathered to share newspapers from their homeland, converse in Spanish, and provide opportunities for their children to meet and mingle. These immigrants were not poverty-stricken and, though Latino by definition, they appeared to others to be a gathering of Europeans. This is not surprising in that many had a common Italian background inherited from their forbears who had emigrated from Italy to Argentina in the nineteenth century.

It was difficult for outsiders in California to sort out who belonged in the Hispanic community. In the opening days of affirmative action programs, those with Spanish surnames were identified as the ones to receive special treatment. When it became obvious that there was a great deal of similarity between the children of Tom Smith and Mary Martínez on the one hand, and Tom Martínez and Mary Smith on the other, the emphasis shifted to identifying Hispanics by their ability to speak Spanish. This also failed because many Hispanics in California do not speak Spanish, and many non-Hispanics do.

Gradually the emphasis shifted to talking about "people of color," but even this presents problems. In the census of 1990 it was possible for people to identify themselves by both dominant background and race. A substantial segment of the population in California identified itself as ethnically of Hispanic background, yet white. Another substantial segment, recalling a Hispanic heritage not considered dominant, had become so assimilated that it had become unrecognizable.

Labels also failed to be enlightening. The term "Chicano," widely used to refer to members of the Hispanic community, technically refers to Mexican-Americans born in the United States; it therefore obviously excludes many immigrants. The term "Latino," technically the equivalent of "Latin American," is equally exclusive.

"Hispanic" has become truly an ethnic term indicating an inherited, shared history. An important way Hispanics are recognized and self-identified is through participation in the interests of the Hispanic community. And what has come to be understood as the "interests" of this community are often activities which are congruent with the fight for just economics, humanitarian rights and social justice by activist Catholics in both the Americas.

Catholics in California have made themselves part of this battle. Building on their experiences of helping Latin American immigrants, Catholics were instrumental in assisting the relocation of Asian refugees after the Vietnam war by providing welfare assistance, language classes and immigration advice. By devoting time and energy to the new arrivals, they also helped to interpret the experiences of these immigrants to the wider community. Focusing on service and justice, these Catholics were part of the larger Catholic community offering prayers each Sunday for those suffering and dying in Latin America.

Latino groups in California remain very cohesive with members passing frequently through Los Angeles International Airport, a situation which caused a visiting Californian in Guatemala to realize that Los Angeles seems to be regarded almost as a northern city of that country. The *New York Times* noted that in many cases in California, Spanish remains the exclusive language of the third generation, an unusual situation for immigrant groups. In these tightly knit communities, Spanish-language newspapers from the homeland circulate, and internal problems of one country are shared with Hispanic immigrants from other places. As part of this sharing, Californian Catholics hear a spectrum of questions being asked by their Hispanic friends.

Why, ask the Nicaraguans, did the Pope insult their revered Spanish-language poet, Ernesto Cardenal, and drive him to tears? Why, ask the Argentineans, does the Vatican have anything to do with torturers and murderers? Why, ask the Brazilians, does the Vatican seem intent on curtailing or eliminating their base communities? When, they worry, will their hierarchy suffer the same suppression as that of the Catholics in Holland? Why, ask the Philippinos, was their beloved Archbishop Sin so coolly received at the Vatican after the ouster of Marcos? Whose side, it is widely asked in California, is the Pope on?

These questions are shared with fellow Catholics outside the Hispanic community who are asking somewhat similar questions of their own. Why was the Archbishop of Seattle, Raymond Hunthausen, humiliated and stripped of much of his power? Was it because of his aggressive posture on social action or because of his leadership in developing the position paper of the American bishops denouncing nuclear war? After the *Los Angeles Times* printed a cartoon by Conrad showing John XXIII standing before an open window welcoming the sunlight in the top panel, and a grumpy John Paul closing the curtains and marching away from the window in the bottom, Catholics had additional questions to answer coming from outside the Catholic community.

At one pole are Catholics who wish to defend the freedom of the American bishops to continue to lead the Catholic Church in the United States. Historian Penny Lernoux says these claim "there is no God-given reason for Rome to exercise absolute authority" and cite church historians and theologians who "argue that papal centralization is of relative recent origin." Though, according to Lernoux, they may "admit that the Vatican can cause them trouble, they contend that the changes brought about by Vatican II are too far advanced to be undone." At the other pole are Catholics who regard all that has happened since Vatican II as a disaster which must be reversed if the Catholic Church is to be saved. In the middle is the largest group, which remains confused.

The challenge of ministering to Hispanic Catholics continues to grow. Since the extension of amnesty to undocumented aliens who have met certain residency requirements, Californian Catholics have provided aggressive assistance to help these most recent immigrants through the maze of naturalization forms, and have assisted in providing the required language and civics instruction necessary to attain citizenship. They also have assisted in providing sanctuary for political refugees from Latin America as well as Spanish-speaking members to act as buffers between the new Latino immigrants and the larger English-speaking society.

When Roger Mahony, previously bishop of Stockton, was appointed archbishop of Los Angeles in 1986, Hispanics and liberals noted with enthusiasm his fluency in Spanish, his leadership in promoting nuclear disarmament, and his circulation of the American bishops' 1983 pastoral letter on peace. Mahony had been raised in the then-semirural San Fernando Valley, had marched with César Chávez, and was reputed to be a strong defendant of immigrant rites. His early move to appoint an Hispanic head of St. John's Seminary in Camarillo was noted with enthusiasm.

More recently Mahony has been criticized for moving in an increasingly conservative direction in which he has failed to capitalize on his position as a potential leader of the Hispanic community. He has been faulted for failing to support the Claretian Father

Luís Oliveres in his use of La Placita as a political sanctuary, for his aggressive action against gravediggers in Catholic cemeteries when they attempted to organize, for supporting activists blocking access to abortion clinics, and for failing to respond to the AIDS crisis. Most important, in the eyes of some critics, is the failure of Mahony's "Latino Aid Plan," which he created with the support of members of United Neighborhood Organization, to redistribute power. In the ironic words of a priest contrasting Mahony with McIntyre, "The old regime is dead. Long live the old regime."

Some saw Mahony's appointment as one more move in John Paul's effort to strengthen Vatican control of the American Catholic Church through his power to appoint bishops committed to centralized, papal authority. In any event, the Pope made known his pleasure in Mahony's performance as archbishop when he raised him to cardinal in June of 1991. At the same time, Mahony made known his understanding of the Archdiocese of Los Angeles as well as the larger American Catholic Church when he used the occasion to call for unity in a divided and increasingly diverse church. He further demonstrated his knowledge of his flock when, in response to a reporter traveling with his entourage to Rome, he named as a favorite food, "take-out" chicken *fajitas* (barbecued chicken in a tortilla).

While the most profound contribution of the Catholics in Southern California to the larger Church in the United States has been and continues to be its creative response to the growing presence of Hispanic Catholics in its midst, the Church in Northern California during the post-Vatican II period was responding to a very different type of challenge. In the 1960s, the human potential movement was initiated in California. It challenged Catholic religious sensibilities, particularly in the area of sexual ethics, and set off a significant chain of events contributing to a resurgence of interest in classical expressions of Catholic spirituality.

FURTHER READING:

Davis, Mike. *City of Quartz*. New York: Verso, 1990.

Ingham, John M. *Mary, Michael and Lucifer: Folk Catholicism in Central Mexico*. Austin: University of Texas Press, 1986.

Lernoux, Penny. *People of God: The Struggle of World Catholicism*. New York: Viking, 1989.

Murray, Paul V. *The Catholic Church in Mexico*. Vol. I. Mexico City, D.F.: Editorial E.P.M., 1965.

Weber, Francis J. *Century of Fulfillment: The Roman Catholic Church in Southern California, 1840-1947*. Mission Hills, California: The Archival Center of the Archdiocese of Los Angeles, 1990.

4 Mysterious Vineyards

There are periods in the history of any civilization when its rest is disturbed, and in such periods the inner life runs near the surface, ordinary people crave mystical experience, there is much odd behavior, and many things seem possible.

—Walter Truett Anderson, *Upstart Spring*

By 1964, California had a Catholic governor, Edmund G. (Pat) Brown. Also, as the second most populous state in the union, it had 17.5 million inhabitants, of which more than 3.5 million were Catholics. In Northern California three additional sees had been established two years earlier in Oakland, Santa Rosa, and Stockton to care for the growth. Then revolutionary forces were unleashed all across America. Shock waves initiated by the Free Speech movement at the University of California in Berkeley moved east. They mingled with waves moving north from the civil rights struggles as well as others moving west as a new interest in expanding consciousness emanated from old Transcendentalist bastions in New England. The national origins quota system was eliminated in 1965 with the amendment of the McCarren-Walter Act; with accelerating immigration from Asia came Asian religions and Asian Catholics, groups which grew in importance in the increasingly pluralistic environment of California.

Meanwhile, a third of a world away, the Second Vatican Council was profoundly affecting Catholic doctrine and practice. The ancient liturgy was modified as the Latin Mass gave way to vernacular celebrations of the Eucharist. Thomist theology, essentially in place since the Council of Trent in the sixteenth century, was opened for reconsideration. Laypersons, including women, were given a more important place in leading the religious life of the Church. Church architecture and decor were modified as dim interiors lit by flickering candles placed before statues gave way to simpler settings. Importantly, the basic authority structure of the Church was challenged by changing views on sexual morality, changes which posed fresh questions for Catholic theologians.

In the 1950s, a few Catholic liberals had made trips to Benedictine and Trappist monasteries where they found the Catholic heritage of the High Middle Ages still preserved and where they mingled with the separated monastics. Many of these liberals were, at the same time, participating in the growing psychological movement exploring group dynamics in which some discovered personal encounter as the deepest reality. In the 1960s, the activities of these few fed into movements involving many, in which California led the way as it nurtured the human potential movement.

In the new atmosphere of freedom after Vatican II, fences built around members of the religious orders, particularly those of women in terms of dress and schedule, began to fall as nuns and brothers increasingly moved from the cloister into the world. Experimentation became permissible, and the human potential movement became one of the powerful forces influencing the Church. This movement, with roots in the humanistic psychology developed in the '50s on the East Coast, had its California genesis in 1962 at a hot springs spa called the Esalen Institute, located on the rocky cliffs bordering the Pacific in the wild and beautiful Big Sur country below Monterey.

Early seminars at Esalen had focused on philosophy and Eastern religions, interests which the founders, Michael Murphy and Richard Price, had shared since meeting at the Institute for Asian Studies in San Francisco in the late '50s. The focus soon shifted, however, and the human potential movement in California was born—its goal to help individuals achieve personal growth and transformation. By holding out the hope of transformation and, subsequently, spiritual or mystical experience, the human potential movement presented itself to many, including Catholics, as a challenging supplement or even alternative to the traditional, institutional experience of the Church.

Psychology, in the form of Freudianism, had already undermined the Catholic concept of mortal sin, which requires the presence of a fully responsible individual who, through acknowledgement of sin and confession, may take the first step toward forgiveness and reconciliation. If the unconscious is in control, as alleged by Freud, that is, if it is the unconscious which acts rather than the conscious will, then the possibility of mortal sin disappears and, with it, a great deal of guilt.

The moral rules of the Church, and its sacrament of reconciliation when these transgressed rules are confessed, was replaced, for some, by self development, with the goal of bringing unconscious forces and conscious will into harmony. In the human potential movement, agents of this self development are often other persons, a situation encouraged by encounter groups that include mutual confession. Encounter groups were also promoted as a way of achieving a new intimacy and community in what was viewed as an increasingly isolating and alienating society.

Among the first to seek a renewed sense of community through these new techniques were the sisters of the Immaculate Heart Order, an order that managed schools in the Archdiocese of Los Angeles. In the fall of 1967, they invited psychologists from the Western Behavioral Sciences Institute in La Jolla to lead encounter workshops. In mid-project, a majority of the nuns voted to leave the formal structure of religious life in the Catholic Church and regroup as a lay order. The shock among Californian Catholics was visible.

Men in the religious orders were free to participate in outside workshops such as those held at the Esalen Institute and its counterparts, including Kairos in Rancho Santa Fe and the Topanga Center in Los Angeles. Jesuits were part of these groups. When Esalen established a residential program in 1967 to supplement the week-long and weekend workshops, a Jesuit was a member of the first residential group. Nearby, in the same year, at the University of Santa Clara, Jesuits termed "highly placed" by Malachi Martin gathered to participate in a worldwide Jesuit effort to recapture the "primitive charism" of their order. The group was charged with choosing the future directions of the Society and developing a system of total Jesuit development.

Meanwhile, in May 1967, *Psychology Today* in Del Mar commenced publication with "Human Potentialities" by Aldous Huxley, reprinted in its first issue. As circulation rapidly climbed above 100,000, news of the developments in California were channeled to other parts of the country. The August issue carried an article by Episcopal Bishop James Pike identifying the human potential movement as a way of reaching disaffected youth. Though ex-Catholic Pike wrote as an Episcopal rather than a Catholic leader, he carried some weight with Catholics, owing to a Vatican II goal of increased Catholic participation in the ecumenical movement through reconciliation with separated Christians. Of these, perhaps the most promising group in America appeared to be the Episcopalians, many of whom, since the high church movement of the nineteenth century, thought of themselves as Catholic, though not Roman Catholic, rather than as Protestant.

Pike identified the vanguard of those rejecting the institutional structure of the Church as the young people, called "hippies" or "flower children," who had taken up residence in the Haight-Ashbury district of San Francisco, committing themselves to preaching joy, non-violence, altruism, and mysticism. He didn't say so, but "the Haight" was also developing as the West Coast center of the adolescent drug culture. Pike also noted that among students at the University of California, the demand for religion courses, including theology, was greater than ever. Pike found the attempt to find answers to "Who am I, and how do I relate to what is ultimate and infinite?" to be the goal of every person's search.

Michael Murphy followed Pike in the December issue with a description of the group phenomenon which he and others were developing at Esalen. He explained that he was willing to explore any approach to reach the domain of senses and feelings, giving that as a reason he had included group leaders as diverse as a Carmelite monk, a Zen scholar, and a Hindu mystic.

An early contributor to *Psychology Today* was Father James Kavanaugh. He had earlier written "I am a Priest, I Want to Marry" for the *Saturday Evening Post*. About the time that he wrote for *Psychology Today*, Kavanaugh resigned from the priesthood, married, and became a counselor at the Human Resources Institute in La Jolla where he had opportunities to join with Southern California leaders of the human potential movement. Later as a clinical psychologist and contemporary poet headquartered in San Francisco and Los Gatos, Kavanaugh became well known as a speaker and seminar leader throughout California. Kavanaugh was not the only Catholic to be publishing radical opinions in the late '60s; voices were being raised everywhere. But his thinking presents an integrated view, and he was influential in California.

In his *Post* article, Kavanaugh argued that celibacy for priests is an ecclesiastical discipline in need of reform. He noted that celibacy was often called a marriage to Christ but said he wanted "to know God in the way that personal human love alone allows." Saying that he was concerned about "the salvation of his own soul," he pointed out that the Catholic Church no longer had a medieval or Victorian view of sex and that he, as a priest, had been called on to teach "the beauty of marriage, sacredness of sex, and the picture of divine friendship contained in the image of married love." Saying that he wanted the love of a wife and not just sex, he concluded that to him, "Heaven is a distant hope, Hell an unreal possibility."

These were the themes he elaborated in *A Modern Priest Looks at his Outdated Church,* which rapidly went through many printings and influenced a large body of opinion. Kavanaugh, through his counselling experience as a priest, had become convinced of the transforming power of married love, which he considered more sacred than the legalistic rules of the Church, such as those forbidding birth control. Kavanaugh considered his own adolescence to have been warped by threats of Hell for unforgiven mortal sins, and he deplored the necessity of counselling Catholics in ways that, in his view, pervert the love of Christ.

In the same year, Kavanaugh predicted others would soon be leaving the priesthood. He was not wrong. Moreover, among priests who elected to stay with the church, there was a marked change in behavior. For example, when the papal encyclical, *Humanae Vitae*, was issued in 1968 containing a strong reiteration of the traditional condemnation of artificial methods of birth control, almost the entire faculty of the Jesuit School of Theology in Berkeley published a joint manifesto denouncing it, thereby departing from the historic loyalty of the order to the pope.

There was evidence that changes were taking place nationwide. A survey conducted by the Catholic sociologist, Father Andrew Greeley, indicated that by 1970 more than four-fifths of the Catholic clergy did not insist on acceptance of the official birth-control teaching in the confessional. Greeley compares this to 1960 when few, if any, priests would have been willing to give absolution to penitents who refused to accede to this teaching.

Justified by changes made by Vatican II, a new position developed that was used to defend the freedom of an informed conscience. If a Catholic has made an honest effort to become informed on the moral teaching of the Church; and if, in good conscience, he or she cannot accede to that teaching; and if the seeker finds a compatible position in the teaching of a Catholic theologian or moral philosopher, then the individual Catholic is free to follow that teaching. This method of reasoning was later condemned by Pope John Paul II. However, there is no evidence that his disapproval made a great impression on the 88 percent of American Catholics who by 1974 had ceased to accept the birth-control teaching of the Church.

Another important conclusion of Greeley's survey was that priests were becoming less active in their recruitment of young men to be priests like themselves. Results were marked. In 1962 there were 55,581 priests and 46,189 seminarians in the United States. By 1988 there were 53,522 priests, (with a much older average age) and 7,510 seminarians.

By 1990, the nationwide problem of a shortage of priests was particularly evident in California. Between 1986 and 1990, the Catholic population of California grew by 1.2 million while the number of priests in the state declined by 368. One result is that the ratio of parishioners to priests in the Archdiocese of Los Angeles is now 2,200 to 1 and worsening. It has become the highest in the nation and almost three times that of the Archdiocese of New York.

The decline in the acceptance of religious vocations was not limited to seminarians. The religious orders also experienced a loss of members and lack of recruits. In the case of orders for nuns and sisters, this decline may be linked not only to changes promoted by the human potential movement but also to a change in a sense of self image, such as that encouraged by Kavanaugh. As recently as 1946, Henry L. Walsh, S.J., had described the work of the religious sisters who pioneered in California as "an offering to their heavenly spouse." Kavanaugh attacked this view by describing the concept of sisters as brides of Christ as a spirituality fashioned before Freud which has grown pathetic and out of date and which, further, is bad theology because Christ took no spouse except the Church.

As recruits for the teaching orders declined, revolutionary changes occurred in the Catholic schools. Between 1960 and 1986, the number of Catholic high schools nationwide dropped from 2,433 to 1,488 while enrollments dropped from approximately 844,000 to 766,000. In terms of actual numbers, California ran counter to the trend by holding steady at 129 Catholic high schools and actually increasing high school enrollments from 55,000 to 74,000.

However, in the same period, Catholic grade school enrollment in California dropped from 248,000 to 177,000. Nationwide Catholic grade school enrollments were cut by more than half. Since Catholic immigration was sizable during this period, it is fair to say that in California, as elsewhere in the nation, the percentage of Catholics attending Catholic schools dropped dramatically. Moreover, those attending were more likely to be taught by lay rather than religious personnel.

Kavanaugh also deplored the mode of dress and rules of convent life that separated the sisters from the humanity they wished to serve. His view was consistent with the new Vatican II emphasis on the Church as the people of God, an emphasis that promised to replace the older concept of the Church as a hierarchical system. A desire to become fully participating members of the group consti-tuting the mystical body of Christ began to take precedence, for many, over a desire for an elevated place within the hierarchy of the institutional system.

Techniques for more fully participating in the world continued to be developed in human growth centers. These techniques were then introduced into convents where young sisters, according to Kavanaugh, were also taught about personal motivation, hidden sources of guilt, and latent fears of sex and marriage. Opening up to such change had its impact: nationwide, between 1966 and 1969, 14,000 Roman Catholic sisters left their convents.

In 1969 the Jesuit leaders who had assembled in Santa Clara two years earlier released their report pointing a new direction for their order that emphasized personal self-discovery, integration, and growth. Obedience was to be replaced by consultation and daily Mass for young Jesuits by professionally directed sensitivity sessions. Further, the report stated, a way should be sought to pro-vide opportunities for Jesuits to have intimate relationships with women, though not involving marriage, formal or common-law.

Beyond his desire for a transforming love and full participation in Catholic religious life, Kavanaugh had, in 1967, expressed a desire for the Catholic Church to participate more fully in the ecu-menical movement. Vatican II had encouraged Catholics to enter into a dialogue with the world, and the presence of Protestants and Jews as observers at the Council had underscored the desire of the hierarchy to heal ancient divisions and schisms. Given this new cli-mate Kavanaugh deplored the priestly requirement that they make every effort to lead non-Catholics to the Truth.

The pluralistic climate of California provided many opportuni-ties for Catholics to meet adherents of other denominations, to enjoy their friendship and eat with them, and, if they responded like Kavanaugh, "to marvel at their sincerity." Kavanaugh insisted that many Catholics no longer wished to regard their new friends as "heretics," "potential converts," or persons "who know but half the truth."

In California, moreover, with the exception of some Hispanic congregations, Catholics had established fewer ethnic "Catholic ghettos"; in other words, places where the Church was the most visible and jealous power in the community. Instead, Catholic leaders in California sought the friendship and advice of religious leaders of other groups. Richard Baker, from 1971 to 1983 the abbot of the San Francisco Zen Center, estimated that during the California governorship of Jerry Brown, (an ex-Jesuit seminarian and son of the earlier Catholic governor Pat Brown), 30 percent of the Governor's advisors were recruited from the Zen ranks. Of course, in California, what actually constituted "Zen ranks" could be interpreted amorphously. The Benedictine member of the Zen Center board of directors, Brother David Steindl-Rast, would likely have identified himself as being also part of the Catholic ranks. But that is the point.

Historian Helen Tworkov notes that the situation in California was fluid and that Baker reflected the intellectual renaissance that California was cultivating. What she finds essentially different was that in California a lot of people were beginning to learn a little about a lot of things, which, when viewed from the East Coast, seemed superficial and intellectually spurious. She terms these people "the eclectic advocates of the New Age," describing them as dedicated pragmatists who take the life of the mind seriously. These pragmatists included Catholics.

The emphasis on pragmatism was important and brought with it an emphasis on practice, an emphasis which touched those who remained within Catholic religious orders as well as those who chose the wider world. The human potential movement had promised something very like salvation through its ability to engineer "peak experiences," the main focus of one of its founders, Abraham Maslow. Eastern religions had been mined for the same purpose, and many Catholics combined the several techniques. At the Immaculate Heart Hermitage, high in the Santa Lucia mountains, the Camaldolese hermits installed a Zendo meditation room in the basement.

In 1968, Father Thomas Merton explored the possibility of establishing a Trappist monastery in the Redwoods of Northern California. He was, at the time, on his way to the First World Spiritual Summit Conference held in Calcutta, sponsored by the Temple of Understanding, an international body of religious leaders. Though Merton was to suffer a fatal accident in Sri Lanka, and the Trappists were not to locate in California, his presence at the Calcutta Conference emphasized the growing contacts between Catholic and Asian religious leaders. A leading center for such contacts was developing in the intellectually and culturally pluralistic community of Berkeley, which houses both the oldest campus of the University of California and the Graduate Theological Union with its eight seminaries, including those of the Jesuits and Franciscans.

By the late 1960s many Catholics were receiving their higher education in environments outside the strict control of the church, unlike the traditional Catholic college or university. But even students at traditional Catholic colleges were experiencing new freedom. The students at the University of Santa Clara, the University of San Francisco, and the Holy Names College in Oakland had access to many of the same opportunities as students at Berkeley and Stanford. These included opportunities to participate in new forms of liturgical worship such as those arranged by Harvey Cox and Corita Kent at the Episcopal Grace Cathedral in San Francisco. Cox and Kent later repeated their California experiment at a discotheque in Boston complete with homemade bread, ushers in beads, and psychedelic strobe lighting provided by Kent.

At the same time, cooperative educational enterprises were developing, such as the one allowing students at the Dominican College at San Rafael to take courses at the Psychosynthesis Institute in San Francisco, an arrangement which collapsed in the late '70s amid charges by its members that the leadership of the Institute was showing signs of developing into a cult. Public lectures were also available, many sponsored by the San Francisco program of the Esalen Institute, by speakers such as Harvey Cox, author of *The Secular City*, which had been widely acclaimed by "Death of God" theologians. Another speaker was Anglican Bishop John A.T. Robinson, whose *Honest to God* (1963) had made public his doubts regarding central Roman Catholic as well as Anglican doctrines. At the same time the Stanford engineering professor, Willis Harmon, was conducting experiments with LSD and publicly referring to the shift of focus on transcendental questions from the philosophical to the empirical as a "Copernican Revolution."

As the '60s drew to a close, California celebrated the bicentennial anniversary of the entrance of Portolá and Serra into California. In 1769, Serra had been commissioned by his superior to "labor in the mysterious vineyards of California." In 200 years, California had not greatly changed. Walter Truett Anderson provided a suggestive description of the Big Sur territory housing Esalen, the Immaculate Heart Hermitage, and the Tassajara Zen Center when he wrote of an "inner life" running near the surface, with "ordinary people" craving "mystical experience" and "much odd behavior," but there were "mysterious vineyards" elsewhere in California as well.

Gradually there was a shift of emphasis in the human potential movement as Esalen, more and more, began to include philosophers, theologians, and religious gurus. Earlier, when Bishop Robinson was invited to come from England, he had emerged from Esalen to speak of exploration into God as a transpersonal experience and as a possible solution to doubt. Cox had come from Harvard and, concluding that his celebration of the secular city had been only a partial truth, had gone on to participate in the growing interest in Eastern religions. Finally, in the late '60s, there was the birth of transpersonal psychology, which had the goal of helping seekers to go beyond the limits of personal growth in order to achieve levels of consciousness long sought by various religions. In 1969, the *Journal of Transpersonal Psychology* commenced publication in Palo Alto and its first issue, a sell-out, had to be reprinted. The search for mystical experience by means other than drugs was on.

Early in the '70s, in an effort to gain understanding of what was going on in the Californian youth culture, sociology Professors Robert Bellah and Charles Glock, of the University of California at Berkeley, initiated an elaborate study of religion in California, choosing this as "the strategic point of entry into the question of contemporary cultural transformations." Religion, they considered, might be the most profound of these transformations.

Nine different groups in the San Francisco Bay area were chosen for participant observation, including a group participating in the Catholic Charismatic renewal. This movement had its origins in 1966 among lay members of the theology faculty at Duquesne who, through their prayer experience, had come to understand themselves as filled with the Holy Spirit. American roots of the Duquesne experience can be found in the Protestant Pentecostal movement radiating from Los Angeles a half century earlier. In the atmosphere of greater freedom encouraged by Vatican II, Catholic Charismatics considered themselves free to seek the same gifts of the spirit as the Protestant Pentecostals. These included speaking in tongues (glossolalia), the capacity for prophecy, and spiritual healing. Though slow to gain acceptance by the hierarchy, numerous priests, brothers, and nuns saw in it a new source of power and renewal. As a result entire parishes, schools, and monasteries became Pentecostal prayer communities.

The monastic traditions also presented themselves, at this time, as an alternative to drugs, for many engaged in an empirical search for God. With renewed interest in monasticism, Catholic retreat centers took on a new importance, and the interest in lay retreats which had earlier been evidenced by Catholic progressives became more widespread. In his introduction to Patricia Christian-Meyer's *Catholic America: Self-Renewal Centers and Retreats* (1989), Brother David Steindl-Rast points to a personal encounter with God as the source of religious vitality and holds that it is the individual's responsibility to become open for that encounter. Referring to Benedictine monasteries in France and Germany as "cold frames in which seedlings awaited the springtime that Pope John XXIII brought to the Church with the Second Vatican Council," he suggests that retreat and renewal centers in America may be the cold frames presently nurturing the vitality of the Church.

Steindl-Rast, a frequent participant at Esalen, was also associated with leaders of the developing New Age movement in its early years. He was a contributor to the Lindisfarne Conferences held in 1974 and 1975 in which many of them participated. Speaking to them at that time, he said that all people are meant to be mystics, and he defined mysticism as the experience of communing with ultimate reality.

Christian-Meyer wrote *Catholic America* in order, in her words, to reconcile her Catholic upbringing with her ten years of Zen training. Claiming that the experiential side of Roman Catholicism had been a taboo topic which had been virtually lost from the six-teenth century until perhaps thirty years ago, she claims she heard nothing about it during the years she attended Roman Catholic schools and a Jesuit college. She quotes Mother Tessa Bielecki as saying she often meets people who

> compare a Sunday-school level grasp of Christianity to sophis-ticated Eastern (i.e. non-Christian) contemplative practices, and it's a totally unfair comparison. They know nothing about Christian mysticism, and so they think there's nothing to it.

Catholic retreat centers are compensating for this lack. There are over forty retreat centers in California associated with the Catholic Church, more than in any other state. Some are oriented toward the silence of a solitary retreat, others toward group experi-ence such as marriage encounter or *cursillo*, an intense encounter-type three day weekend. The resident brothers and sisters at the retreat centers share many of their meals and their religious devo-tions and often provide counselling and spiritual direction.

One major retreat center in California is the Santa Sabina Cen-ter run by the Dominican Sisters of San Rafael adjacent to the Dominican College campus. It is typical in that it encourages a con-templative way of being, but atypical in that it welcomes groups as varied as those from the Presbyterian San Francisco Theological Seminary, Visalia Methodist Church, and Insight Meditation West, based on the Vipassana variety of Buddhist meditation. In choos-ing this ecumenical approach, the Dominican sisters of San Rafael are no doubt aware that the results of prayer and meditation can be as surprising as the following experience reported by Christian-Meyer.

> I was sitting in a silent retreat, meditating, when I heard a bell carillon in the distance pealing out a medley of lovely hymns to Mary—hymns that had been engraved on my heart when I was a small child in a Roman Catholic school. Suddenly the room seemed bathed in blinding light and I felt an overwhelming

sense of love and joy far beyond the mere human emotions I had experienced all too briefly in my life. . . .

I suddenly found myself praying fervently to God, something I had not done in many years. I still don't much understand what really happened. I felt so very much at peace, and yet I was acutely uncomfortable. This was, after all, the third day of a very intensive Zen Buddhist retreat.

The resurgence of interest in Catholic monasticism in the '70s was associated with the developing transpersonal movement. Esalen increasingly designed programs to help seekers achieve levels of consciousness long sought by various religions and practices with this goal were available elsewhere. Interest was widespread. As early as the end of the '60s, Stanford had introduced a lecture course on the practice of meditation, which attracted 350 students the first time it was offered. Other California campuses had provided similar opportunities. Harmon had observed that students "in the millions at least," were involved with "awareness-expanding" activities. The search for ways to expand consciousness was dominated, at this time, by Eastern religions. A concurrent survey done in the San Francisco Bay area had found fifteen groups teaching meditation, of which fourteen were explicitly based on techniques of Eastern religions.

The early emphasis on Eastern religions was defended by claims that the Western tradition of meditation is "sketchy" and that there is a Western tendency to focus on explanation rather than experience. The practice of Buddhist meditation was described by Thomas Merton as developing a kind of consciousness that is "above and beyond description." At the same time, Christianity was described as emphasizing prayers of petition rather than the higher kind of prayer that seeks only spiritual gifts or union with God. Soon, Catholics who did not agree with this assessment began to be heard.

In 1973, a series of lectures sponsored by the Esalen Institute was held in San Francisco. Representatives of various forms of traditional spirituality described as being in contact with the practical, "mystical" heart of ancient teachings were invited to speak.

William Johnston, S.J., speaking on "Christianity in Dialogue with Zen," and Dom Aelred Graham, a Benedictine from England speaking on "Contemplative Christianity," were included. In his preface to the published lectures, Jacob Needleman, head of the Center for the Study of New Religions at Berkeley, observed that experiments with meditation, other religious techniques, and attempts at self-exploration and human relations through sensory awareness, encounter, and communes had, by this time, spread throughout the world.

By the '80s, interest in the revitalization of Catholicism brought about by various forms of spirituality spread beyond the earlier interest in monasticism. However, the focus continued to be on the experiential. Joseph P. Chinnici, O.F.M., gives a vivid picture of the experiential and pluralistic face of Californian Catholicism in his description of a 1983 Good Friday service at St. Boniface Church in San Francisco, which he terms "a new and fuller expression" of Catholic spirituality.

> Imagine the "people of God" gathered together. Some, dressed impeccably, have left their downtown businesses on Market Street to spend an hour in prayer; others, reflecting the hungry eyes and ragged lives of more permanent residents, have pushed and crowded for their places inside the spacious, gilded interior of the Church. They are all present in one body: the rich and the poor; old and young; male and female; cleric and lay; Protestant and Catholic; White, Black, Hispanic and Asian. Ringed by cross and candle, acolytes winding their way around the nave's dark edges and pausing fourteen times to commemorate some place in the world where the Lord is daily tortured, these people rise and fall together, exchanging "misereres" for their sins. Later in the service, they abandon their pews and jostle each other in a slow, pained procession of humanity prostrating itself before the image of the crucified Christ.

As the decade developed, the publishing business found that millions of Americans were buying books on spirituality, an amazing 37 million were purchased in 1985 alone. Publishers responded by reissuing Catholic classics, while academic divisions for the study of spirituality were established at the Graduate Theological Union in Berkeley, Fordham, Duquesne, and the Gregorian University in Rome. Sandra Schneiders, I.H.M., a member of the faculty at the Jesuit Seminary in Berkeley, speaking at a national seminar, described the term "spirituality" as historically Catholic. Yet, she said,

> It is truly remarkable that a term, which only twenty years ago connoted suspect enthusiasm or mindless piety in Protestant circles, and was virtually unknown to Judaism, Eastern traditions, Native American religion, the new religious movements, or secular systems of life integration, is now used freely within all of these circles.

Schneiders defines "spirituality" as "the experience of consciously striving to integrate one's life in terms not of isolation and self-absorption but of self-transcendence toward the ultimate value one perceives." Her broad definition goes beyond understanding "spirituality" simply in terms of mysticism, which Schneiders finds to be a normal development in the life of faith rather than an extraordinary state to which only some are invited. Rather Schneiders' definition permits including social activism as a form of "spirituality."

Schneiders presents an understanding of "spirituality" which goes far beyond that discussed by Marsha Sintar in the widely read Paulist Press publication, *Ordinary People as Monks and Mystics*. Sintar, who heads a human resource development firm based in Santa Rosa, returns to the '60s model by describing her book as being about self-actualizing and self-actualized people who detach from society because of a strong preference, even a need, for privacy to make possible a response to an inner call. A tension remains, in Californian Catholicism, between those who seek self-transcendence by reaching outward to others, the world, and ultimate values, and those who primarily seek the inner call.

Since Vatican II, Californian Catholicism has developed in an increasingly pluralistic environment during successive decades influenced first by the human potential movement, then by transpersonal concerns and a resurgence of interest in monasticism; and, finally, by a broader interest in other forms of spirituality. In the course of this development, it has exhibited the freedom, curiosity, and exuberance characteristic of Californians in general. The influence of Catholic monasticism during this period on Catholics as well as non-Catholics was and continues to be consistent with the widespread interest in the spiritual practices of other religions. However, it also reflects an historic tension, evident in California since colonial days, between the regular and the secular clergy, that is between the members of the religious orders and those more closely participating in the hierarchical organization responsible for protecting the magisterium and mythic boundaries of the Church.

In the decades following Vatican II, the freedom and increasing pluralism of California were impacting not only Catholic practices but also Catholic doctrine. During this period, Californian Catholics made significant contributions not only to spiritual practices but also to discussions surrounding the magisterium or teachings of the Church concerning its history and beliefs.

FURTHER READING:
Anderson, Walter Truett. *Upstart Spring: Esalen and the American Awakening.* Reading, Massachusetts: Addison-Wesley, 1983.
Christian-Meyer, Patricia. *Catholic America: Self-Renewal Centers and Retreats.* Santa Fe, New Mexico: John Muir Publications, 1989.
Kavanaugh, James. *A Modern Priest Looks at his Outdated Church.* New York: Trident Press, 1967.
McNamara, William, O.C.D. "Psychology and the Christian mystical tradition," in Charles Tart, *Transpersonal Psychologies.* New York: Harper & Row, 1975.
Steindl-Rast, Brother David. "The monk in us," in Michael Katz, William P. Marsh, and Gail Gordon Thompson (eds.), *Earth's Answer: Explorations of Planetary Culture at the Lindisfarne Conferences.* New York: Harper & Row, Lindisfarne Books, 1977.
Toolan, David. *Facing West from California's Shores: A Jesuit's Journey into New Age Consciousness.* New York: Crossroad, 1987.
Tworkov, Helen. *Zen in America.* Berkeley, California: North Point Press, 1989.

5 Mythic Boundaries

*The Californians are a singularly inquisitive and intelligent race.
Everybody is able to read and write; and even the common
labourer has his morning newspaper brought every day of his life
to his cottage door. They wish to learn the why of everything, and
they are little inclined to take anything upon a mere "ipse dixit."
They love knowledge, and desire to obtain it easily, so they are
great frequenters of lectures and sermons; and will go anywhere
to hear them when they believe them to be good.*
　　　　—Herbert Cardinal Vaughan, *The Dublin Review,* 1866

*Since Pioneer days, California has served as the test range for
America's mythic boundaries.*
　　　　—David Toolan, S.J., *Facing West From California's Shores,* 1987

Americans pioneering west to Oregon and California spoke of
all the vast territory beyond the continental divide as the Pacific
Slope and saw the western shore of the Pacific as the final boundary of their pilgrimage. Californians still commonly refer to themselves as westerners and speak of living on the "West Coast."
Gradually, however, an intuition of another sort is also taking
hold. Californians increasingly think of themselves as residents on

the eastern edge of the Pacific basin. Culturally they find themselves to be part of that great complex of countries constituting the Pacific Rim and this location increasingly influences the definition of the ground upon which Californians stand.

One consequence of this changing definition, as suggested in the previous chapter, is that more opportunities are present for all Californians to share in the increasing religious pluralism of their state. At the same time, California remains the intellectual center for the cluster of states west of the Rocky Mountains. One result of these two senses of location is that Californian Catholics find themselves to be participants in the religious pluralism of the Pacific Rim as well as in the intellectual centers of the Pacific Slope. Their participation brings intellectual challenges to Catholicism in California from two directions. On the one hand, as the presence of other religions has sparked a renewed interest in Catholic spirituality, there has developed a greater desire on the part of both Catholics and non-Catholics to understand the foundations of Roman Catholicism. On the other, Californian Catholics, exercising their post-Vatican II freedom to broadly participate in academic and other intellectual circles, are increasingly engaging in biblical scholarship which challenges basic Catholic doctrine.

Before Vatican II, the processes were essentially in place for conveying the magisterium, the official teaching of the Church. A parochial school education, attendance at a Catholic college or university, the sermons at Sunday Mass, the diocesan newspaper all contributed to Catholic intellectual serenity from the cradle to the grave. The sixties ended all that.

As already noted, Bishop John A.T. Robinson's *Honest to God*, published in 1963, raised almost every Christian doctrine for reconsideration. For Catholic Christians, the Second Vatican Council, which began a year earlier, permitted new freedom for just such intellectual inquiry. For instance, no longer did Catholic professors on Catholic campuses have to take a yearly oath denouncing Modernism. Instead they rapidly moved to participate in the historical-critical study of biblical texts. Gone too was the requirement that scholarly research be submitted to the Vatican for approval before publication. At the same time, an increasing number of Catholics received their education in secular institutions, sometimes making them more informed than their parents and parish priests about the theological change.

In the early sixties, a popular philosophy discussed on college campuses and elsewhere was Existentialism, the view that persons, through their own choices, create their own lives. The essential core of an individual, in this view, is self created, not a soul created by God with the purpose that it enjoy Him forever. With Existentialism came Nihilism, the belief that traditional values and beliefs are unfounded, that existence is purposeless and meaningless. The historical-critical study of biblical texts coupled with the philosophies of Existentialism and Nihilism had a strong effect on questioning minds. The rivers of turmoil already flowing in California well before *Honest to God* and Vatican II began flooding.

The previous chapter has already detailed one response that had an early grip in California. Against the charge that God is dead came the response that this is not true if He is experienced as living. Experience ruled the day, and religious experience was where you found it. Given the deep suspicion of Christianity in the sixties, however, Californians, including Californian Catholics, increasingly found their experience outside their church.

Next came the insight that the critical element is not the experience itself but rather the practice accompanying that experience. As discussed in the previous chapter, for many in California the practice of one or another Eastern religion proved attractive, but for many others came a renewed interest in the practices of Christianity, and particularly the spirituality nurtured by the Catholic monastic tradition. While interest developed in the histories, philosophies, and doctrines accompanying various non-Christian religious practices, renewed interest also developed in the foundations of Christianity.

This renewed interest coincided with the discovery of exciting new texts in Israel and Egypt which illuminate the New Testament portion of the Christian canon, the books accepted as authoritative since the early centuries of Christianity concerning the life and death of Jesus and the founding of the Church. For Catholics, the canon consists of the Old Testament, i.e. the Hebrew Bible, plus the

Old Testament Apocrypha, additional texts included in the Greek or Septuagint translation of the Hebrew Bible, as well as the New Testament. The Old and New Testaments, terms which mean the old and new covenants, have been accepted as authoritative by all of orthodox Christianity.

The new discoveries have led also to renewed study of the New Testament apocrypha and pseudepigrapha, terms meaning "hidden" and "falsely written" (i.e., "falsely attributed" and, therefore, without authoritative foundation), texts such as the Gospel of Mary and the Acts of Peter. These texts did not become authoritative and make their way into the canon but were accepted as sacred by many early Christians. This new study of the New Testament apocrypha has thus reopened old issues long labeled heresy by the Catholic magisterium. In combination with other trends surfacing in California, such study has put portions of the Catholic doctrine at risk and invites further change.

Scholars at Catholic universities participate in the study of both the canonical and apocryphal texts. The University of Santa Clara, in operation since 1850, is linked to other Jesuit institutions including Loyola Marymount University in Los Angeles and the University of San Francisco. The diocese of San Diego along with the Religious of the Sacred Heart operate the University of San Diego. In addition, there are the Jesuit and Franciscan seminaries connected to the Graduate Theological Union as well as the seminaries operated by the Archbishoprics of Los Angeles and San Francisco. However, some of the most significant Catholic scholarship is being influenced by studies conducted in two institutions independent of the official Catholic scholarly network—the Center for Antiquity and Christianity in Claremont, and the Westar Institute in Sonoma.

The Center for Antiquity and Christianity, part of the Claremont Graduate School, shares professors with the Claremont School of Theology. The school is the graduate arm of a consortium of independent undergraduate institutions originally founded by the Congregationalists with their establishment of Pomona College. The Claremont School of Theology was originally a Methodist seminary located in Los Angeles until it moved to Claremont to become the leading liberal Protestant seminary in Southern California.

The Center for Antiquity and Christianity is headed by James M. Robinson, who supervised the translation and editing of the gnostic Nag Hammadi tractates found hidden in a cave in Upper Egypt in 1945. These tractates were written in Coptic and probably hidden around 400 C.E. to protect them from an order by the Archbishop of Alexandria to destroy all heretical texts in the monasteries of Egypt. If this is correct, then they were hidden during the period when Roman Orthodoxy was gaining ascendancy over an Alexandrian form of Christian Gnosticism which was earlier dominant in Egypt.

In the Nag Hammadi tractates, the ubiquitous figure of Sophia (Greek for "wisdom") appears. Sophia was already known to biblical scholars from Proverbs where she speaks of herself as created by God, "at the beginning of his work, the first of his acts of old"(8:22). She continues, "I was beside him, like a master workman, and I was daily his delight, rejoicing before him always, rejoicing in his inhabited world and delighting in the sons of man" (8:30-31).

The figure of Sophia has been controversial in Roman Catholicism. The great church of Santa Sophia in Constantinople built in the sixth century, for example, is dedicated to the Person of Christ as Holy Wisdom. Yet there is evidence of other memories as to who constitutes Holy Wisdom. The schism in 1054 from Roman Catholicism was partly caused by the Greek Orthodox unwillingness to add "and the Son" to the creedal statement that the Holy Spirit proceeds from the Father. An objection, registered at the time, was that a son proceeds from a mother, not a mother from a son. The Nag Hammadi documents provide evidence that gnostic Christians in Egypt held Sophia in high regard. An apocryphal gospel, the Gospel of the Hebrews which circulated in Alexandria, records that Jesus referred to Sophia as his mother.

Matthew Fox, a Dominican scholar, who heads the Institute in Culture and Creation Spirituality located at Holy Names College in Oakland is one Californian Catholic interested in Sophia. He is a popular speaker but was silenced for a year by the Vatican for his teachings. Active again, in 1988 he published *The Coming of the Cosmic Christ*, a compilation of his lectures over the previous ten years. He begins his study of the Cosmic Christ with the figure of Sophia.

The interest in Sophia coincides with a rising interest in feminism in California by women seeking new feminine role models. The figure of Sophia has been found attractive by many women, including Catholic women. She provides an alternative to feminists restudying goddess religions considered more primordial than the patriarchal religions such as Christianity, with its doctrine of the Trinity (i.e. God in three male persons, Father, Son, and Holy Spirit). For some she is also more appealing than witches with self-professed supernatural powers, sometimes borrowed from Native American traditions, such as those sought by the self-identified witch, Starhawk, who also operates out of Holy Names College, giving workshops and leading seminars.

This interest in Sophia is typical of the type of theological challenge faced by Catholicism in California where, in the words of Cardinal Vaughan more than a century earlier, people "will go anywhere" to hear a lecture or a sermon in their wish "to learn the *why* of everything." The problem for Californian Catholics is that such inquiry opens doors that, in the extreme religious pluralism of California, may be doors that the Church prefers to keep shut.

Californian Catholics are intellectually challenged by more than religious pluralism and the latest biblical scholarship. Book clubs are popular and university lectures well attended. An example of an academic study providing a doctrinal challenge which Catholics must face in educated circles in California can be found by returning to the ethno-historical study cited in the third chapter.

In his study of the folk Catholicism of Mexico, Ingham found "reproduction" to be the root metaphor, that is the metaphor of fundamental importance. In connection with his consideration of this metaphor, Ingham discusses the difficulties in Tlayacapán brought about for the women attempting to maintain the ideal of the asexual relationship in marriage. He argues that by holding up the relationship of Mary and Joseph as the ideal, as opposed to the fallen relationship of Adam and Eve, the Catholic Church has created an environment which glorifies the role of women as mother at the expense of her role as a full participant in the sexual relationship of marriage. This has resulted, he suggests, in damage to her health and her turning to Mexican cults of spiritism for a satisfaction that is not available to her in marriage.

Noting that in Tlayacapán men are permitted the outlet of prostitutes and extra-marital relations, Ingham points out that "demonic affliction" affects women more than men and that women often seek a cure through *grancieros*. These involve women in ritual activities that include trances and euphoric experiences brought about by various means, including sweat baths. Anyone even reasonably acquainted with the lush landscape of California since the sixties will be able to find parallels in hot tubs, altered states of consciousness, male-led cults with primarily female devotees, trance channeling, ecstatic behavior in Charismatic movements, and female role model confusion. By linking his observations on Tlayacapán to the Catholic doctrine of the perpetual virginity of Mary, Ingham is, of course, directly challenging Catholic sexual ethics and the Church's most important feminine role model who, with Christ, is the co-redemptrix of humanity. Sophia provides an alternative.

The Nag Hammadi documents add greatly to scholars' understanding of how Sophia functioned in Egyptian Christian circles before orthodoxy was established. Sophia appears as both a supreme (higher Sophia) and as a fallen (lower Sophia) figure to whom Christ appears in a redemptive role. A leading scholar of Gnosticism, Kurt Rudolph, suggests that in one of the texts, "Thunder: The Perfect Mind," the two Sophias reflect the soul in two manners of existence: on the one hand as a perfect, divine, and redeeming power; on the other, as a fallen phenomenon exposed to deficiency. Sophia is presented as saying the following.

I am the honored / and the despised.
I am the prostitute / and the respectable woman.
I am the wife / and the virgin.
I am the mother / and the daughter.
I am the members of my mother.
I am the silence / which is unattainable.

The insight [*epinoia*], / which much in the world recalls.
I am the voice, whose sound is manifold,
and the logos/ which has many images.

That all this skirts Catholic heresy, where it is not downright heretical, is obvious. Yet, the *Nag Hammadi Library*, originally published in 1977, has gone through many printings, has recently been revised and expanded, and presents a group of texts to which Catholic theologians are being forced to respond.

Challenging scholarship of another variety is emanating from the Westar Institute in Sonoma, headquarters for the Jesus Seminar led by Robert Funk, in which Protestant and Catholic scholars have been participating since 1985. Searching for the actual words of the historical Jesus through rigorous biblical scholarship, scholars use an approach they term "methodological skepticism" in which evidence is sifted, and quotations which do not pass critical tests are rejected.

The critical tests are the culmination of over a century of historical/critical study of biblical texts to which have been added techniques of other disciplines such as sociology, anthropology, and ethnology. Biblical scholars have long considered that the authors of the gospels of Matthew and Luke had the gospel of Mark at their disposal, as well as a lost document containing a collection of the sayings of Jesus, which they refer to as "Q" for *"Quelle"* or "source" in German. This hypothesis, known as the two-document hypothesis, was reinforced with the discovery among the Nag Hammadi documents of a set of sayings with a gnostic slant called the Gospel of Thomas, previously only known through papyrus fragments.

Many of the sayings in the Gospel of Thomas parallel or reproduce sayings in the hypothetical "Q" and, in certain cases, are considered to be more original. Using the Gospel of Thomas as well as other apocryphal texts originally excluded from the New Testament, scholars from around the country are attempting to reconstruct the original Greek text of "Q." With the leadership of Robinson and other scholars at the Institute for Antiquity and Christianity, the portions of Matthew and Luke considered to be derived from "Q" are being examined word by word, including the Sermon on the Mount of Matthew and the Sermon on the Plain of Luke, which are probably the portions of the hypothetical 'Q' most familiar to Christians.

Scholars at the Westar Institute at Sonoma are using the "Q" research as well as the latest scholarship resulting from the discovery of a second group of texts, also long hidden in jars, called the Qumran texts, or the Dead Sea Scrolls. Scholarship on the scrolls has recently been accelerated by the Huntington Library in San Marino, which has made available to scholars photographs of previously unpublished scroll fragments.

These scrolls are a portion of a library of a monastic Jewish sect of the first century that were discovered at Qumran beside the Dead Sea in 1947. Subsequently, other scrolls were found. With the exception of the Book of Esther, the collection now comprises portions or complete texts of all the books in the Hebrew Bible, which includes the books of the Catholic Old Testament without the Apocrypha. The Qumran documents, placed on scrolls several hundred years earlier than other early transmissions of biblical texts, attest to the accuracy of the early Hebrew scribes.

The Qumran documents are also important in that they reveal the existence of an apocalyptic Jewish sect preparing for the final battle between the forces of good and evil. The group, in many ways, may have been similar to the apocalyptic Jewish community giving birth to Christianity, the circle of followers which first gathered about Jesus. We know something about the Jesus group from the Gospels, the first four books of the New Testament that tell the life of Jesus.

Scholars connected with the Westar Institute have been meticulously examining the New Testament, particularly the four Gospels, as well as related apocryphal texts, in an attempt to recreate the actual words and deeds of the historical Jesus. In *The Historical Jesus* (1991), John Dominic Crossan, Professor of Biblical Studies at the Roman Catholic DePaul University in Chicago, describes his method which is similar to that of other scholars working with the Jesus Seminar. First, Crossan attempts to date the sources of sayings of Jesus and arranges them in a chronological stratification moving

from the earliest to the latest. Then he looks for multiple attesta-
tions, that is, two or more sources, both canonical and non-canoni-
cal, which record the saying. To promote scholarly rigor, he does
not include sayings that are reproduced in only one source even
when, for other reasons, he considers the saying actually to be the
words of Jesus. Finally, he attempts to distinguish the "core" of the
original saying from any later elaborations. Crossan's search for the
historical Jesus thus begins with thirteen pages of sayings he considers original, which he then attempts to understand by locating
their utterance in the Mediterranean world inhabited by Jesus and
his followers.

It is generally agreed that Jesus was born during the reign of
Herod the Great, who died in 4 B.C.E. (i.e., before the common era),
his mother was Mary, and she had a husband named Joseph. He
had several brothers and sisters whom Catholics hold to be children of Joseph by a former marriage.

His public ministry began with an encounter with John the Baptist, and on this occasion, it is recorded, the Spirit of God descended
on him "like a dove." Scholars agree that the earthly ministry of
Jesus took place mainly in Galilee, a province to the north of Judea
and Samaria, where he preached that the Kingdom of God is at
hand. The earliest Christians remembered Jesus as a teacher, healer,
and exorcist, with power over demons and the ability to bind Satan.
The Gospels picture Jesus as a homeless, wandering prophet who,
traveling with a few disciples, addressed crowds in the Jewish villages where he stayed. They record that he chose twelve of his disciples, known to Catholics as the apostles, to carry his message. He
included the outcasts of society in his circle and, challenging the ritual law, emphasized the moral commandments of the Hebrew religion including the injunctions to love God and love one's neighbor.

The Gospels suggest that his followers had come to see Jesus as
the "suffering servant" prophesied in Isaiah who, suffering and
giving his life for others, is justified and exalted. They indicate
Jesus was indicted by the Roman prefect responsible for keeping
the peace, Pontius Pilate, because he was causing disturbances at
the temple. They record that Jesus was condemned and crucified
with two other men and that over his cross was placed the written

indictment, "The King of the Jews" (Mark 15:26). As many of the Jews were anticipating a messiah, an anointed king to lead them against the Romans, the inscription suggests that Jesus was crucified as a messianic pretender. After his death, his body was removed from the cross and placed in a tomb.

Two types of narratives known as "appearance narratives" and "empty tomb narratives" relate what happened after that. In an appearance narrative, an early apostle named Paul relates what he knows of the post crucifixion appearances of Jesus as this information has been conveyed to him. First, Paul says, Jesus appeared to his disciple Peter, then to his brother James, then to others, and finally, Paul claims, to him. The Gospel of Mark contains one of the earliest of the "empty tomb" narratives which relates how, when his followers went to the tomb to anoint the body of Jesus as was the Jewish custom, they found the tomb empty.

Followers of Jesus in Jerusalem anticipated that Jesus would return as the Messiah, to lead them in the messianic age to come, and would defend them at the time of ultimate judgment. Some continued to participate in temple sacrifice but also engaged in house worship which involved partaking of bread and wine, a meal which developed into the Eucharist, the most important Catholic sacrament, and the central event in the Catholic Mass.

The most important leaders of the early community in Jerusalem were the apostles Peter and James, the brother of Jesus. The Acts of the Apostles, the fifth book of the New Testament, which records the history of the birth of the church, reports dissension over the importance of temple sacrifice in the Jerusalem community between the Aramaic-speaking followers of Jesus (who also spoke Aramaic, a language closely related to Hebrew) and those speaking Greek. One of the leaders of the Greek-speaking Jews, Stephen, was stoned to death and the others fled, many of them to Antioch, the Greek capital of the province of Syria to the north. It was here that gentiles, or non-Jews, were first welcomed into their community and that they were first called Christians. Peter, at first, remained with the group in Jerusalem but he later joined the Christians in Antioch.

Preserved in the New Testament are letters which Paul wrote, probably beginning in 51 C.E., to churches which he, along with other missionaries from the church in Antioch, established in Asia Minor, Macedon, and Greece. An axis of orthodoxy stretching from Antioch to Rome, which included the Greek and Macedonian churches, began to develop and eventually evolved into the orthodoxy of Roman Catholicism. Further, even though the Gospel of John and the letters of Paul show gnostic influences, the Antioch–Rome axis generally developed in opposition to a Christian Gnosticism evident in a second axis, stretching from Edessa in Eastern Syria to Alexandria in Egypt, that was later labeled heretical by the orthodox Christians.

In his letters, Paul opposed demands that gentile converts observe the Jewish ritual laws pertaining to circumcision and animal sacrifice, holding, instead, that the sacrifice on the Cross was sufficient to reconcile Christians with God. According to Paul, the old ritual "works" of the Hebrew religion were no longer required. Paul urged Christians to understand and recognize that they live in two ages, both this age and the age to come, which began with the cross. As members of this age, they are still subject to mortality and sin even though, as members of the age to come, they are the beneficiaries of divine power. For Paul, Jesus is a divine being who acts through the Holy Spirit and through whom God acts.

According to Catholic tradition, the apostles took the news of Jesus throughout the known world. Each area looked to a different apostle as the one who brought the *Evangelium*, or Good News, to them. For example, The Acts of the Apostles reports how Philip gave it to an Ethiopian. Christians in eastern Syria looked to the apostle Thomas. It is on Peter that early Christians in Rome came to rely.

As the era began to come to a close when the followers of Jesus were guided by the apostles and wandering prophets, there needed to be new leaders and their authority needed to be guaranteed. Two sources of authority arose. First there was the prophetic authority of the Holy Spirit, understood to have descended at Pentecost and to be present in the gathered church. Second there was the apostolic authority transmitted to certain persons by virtue of their office through the laying on of hands.

By the early second century, church leadership was being exercised by bishops, elders, and deacons. On the death of a bishop, a new one was chosen and authority was transferred to him by the laying on of the hands of the other bishops, continuing, according to Catholic doctrine, an unbroken chain leading from the apostles. Eusebius, an historian of the Church in the fourth century, records that Peter, as the first bishop, inaugurated the chain of authority in both Antioch and Rome. Importantly, for Catholics, the Gospel of Matthew also records that Jesus said to Peter,

> . . . you are Peter, and on this rock I will build my church. . . . I will give you the keys of the kingdom of heaven, and whatever you bind on earth shall be bound in heaven and whatever you loose on earth shall be loosed in heaven. (Matt. 16:18-19)

As this saying has only a single attestation, it falls outside the scope of Crossan's study, *The Historical Jesus*.

Most Catholic scholars would agree with what is included in this brief summary. By the 1990s there had developed a large agreed-upon body of scholarly opinion, both Catholic and Protestant, concerning the origins of Christianity and a growing literature discussing its theological implications. Disagreement is more likely to arise over what has been left out, such as the claim that Mary was a virgin when Jesus was born, a doctrine with biblical support, or the claim that she was a perpetual virgin, a doctrine that relies on tradition and apocryphal texts. Further, the issue of how these questions are to be decided is, itself, an issue. More than a century has elapsed since Vaughan observed that Californians are little inclined to accept the truth, on this and related issues, simply on the basis of a mere *ipse dixit* (i.e., "he himself has said it"). In the intervening years not a lot has changed.

Further, when considering what has been left out when it comes to developing their own spiritual practices, Californian Catholics are confronted with more than issues of biblical scholarship and church doctrine. As members of a pluralistic society located on the Pacific Rim, they are widely confronted with texts reflecting foreign lands and religions and asked to judge if these texts convey spiritual truth. If texts are broadly construed to include persons and rituals, as is frequently done, and if theology is understood as reflection and comment on texts, then what responsibility do Catholic theologians have to reflect and comment on texts not part of the Catholic tradition, and to lead discussions, perhaps at Catholic ashrams, involving Catholic yogis and Catholic Zen masters? This is a central question for Catholic theologians, and Californian Catholics are at the forefront of those who raise it.

In a speech at the University of Southern California in 1986, then-Archbishop and now-Cardinal Mahony held that theology has a critical and creative role to play in grappling with new and unsettled questions. His topic was dissent and his conclusion was that because of the apostolic origin of the Church, dissent remains mere "opinion" while the teaching of the magisterium is "church doctrine." However, more is at stake in California than the doctrinal boundaries of the magisterium. Californian Catholics live within geographical, doctrinal and mythic boundaries and all are important for determining Californian Catholicism within their state.

When considering mythic boundaries, Catholics begin with what Andrew Greeley calls the "Catholic Myth." Myth in this sense should not be contrasted with either "truth" or "history." Rather a "myth" for Greeley is that which binds loyalty and confers identity. By the Catholic Myth, Greeley means that Catholics "imagine God as present in the world and the world as revelatory instead of bleak." Further, by imagining God, Greeley does not mean that God is a figment of their imagination. Rather he means that the Catholic perception of God governs their perception of the world and the ability of the Church to support that perception is the most fundamental reason that Catholics remain Catholic.

The insights of Crossan and the Jesuit, David Toolan, add to Greeley's understanding. For Crossan the crucial element in discovering the sayings of the historical Jesus is that they provide a "score to be played," the basis for a plan of action in a world perceived as sacred. For Toolan what is central is self-perception, noting that many of the growth therapies originally targeted a false self, by which he means the self-created self, the masks and poses of the Existentialists. "Once that gave way," he observed, "the 'rushes' which followed often filled the room with radiance."

By going on to say that California acts as a "test range for America's mythic boundaries," Toolan points to the importance of mythic understandings and the significance of what is included within mythic boundaries. For him, a myth is "the expression in image-language and narrative form of some portion of the wisdom of the race." If understanding mythic boundaries means identifying the scope of the story in terms of which a person perceives self and world, as well as finding the meaning of that story, then since the sixties the mythic boundaries of California have been exploding and Californian Catholics have not been unaffected.

From the beginning California has provided a mythic boundary for many who do not reside within its borders. Mysterious vineyards, the Garden of Eden, the goal of pilgrimage, these are part of the California myth. Yet, at the same time, California is a real place and Catholics dwell within it. Through the last three turbulent decades, the orderly rhythms of Catholic parish life have been maintained. James Hennesey quotes a British professor who participated for fourteen years in a Catholic parish in California during this explosive period and paid his parish the ultimate compliment. Commenting on its prayer life, liturgy, and bible groups as well as its ecumenical contacts and outreach to the sick, needy, and troubled, he termed it the "best community he had ever had the good fortune to live in." These are the Californian Catholics. As they increasingly engage in the inter-religious dialogue developing on the Pacific Rim, as they wrestle with their own personal beliefs and Catholic doctrine, and as they live out their understanding of their faith in their parish communities, they are influencing Catholicism worldwide and helping to prepare their church for the twenty-first century and third millennium.

FURTHER READING:

Crossan, John Dominic. *The Historical Jesus.* San Francisco: Harper & Row, 1991.

Goergen, Donald J. *The Mission and Ministry of Jesus.* Wilmington, Delaware: Michael Glazier, 1986.

Hennesey, James J., S.J. *American Catholics: A History of the Roman Catholic Community in the United States.* New York: Oxford University Press, 1981.

Koester, Helmut. "Introduction to the New Testament." Vol. II. *History and Literature of Early Christianity.* Philadelphia: Fortress Press, 1982.

Meier, John P. *A Marginal Jew: Rethinking the Historical Jesus.* New York: Doubleday, 1991.

Robinson, James M. *The Nag Hammadi Library.* 3rd rev. ed. San Francisco: Harper & Row, 1988.

Rudolph, Kurt. *Gnosis,* translation edited by Robert McLachlan Wilson. New York: Harper & Row, 1983.

Toolan, David, S.J. *Facing West from California's Shores.* New York: Crossroad, 1987.

6 Bibliographic Essay

The orthodox claim of Roman Catholicism is that from the beginning the teaching and doctrine of Christianity has always been everywhere the same. Eusibius wrote *The History of the Church* in the fourth century to support this view. Walter Bauer challenged it in *Orthodoxy and Heresy in Earliest Christianity*, published in German in 1934 and in English in 1971. Bauer finds evidence of early regional differences and argues that Roman Catholicism was only gradually established as the orthodox doctrine.

The claim that American Catholicism and Californian Catholicism represent regional forms of Roman Catholicism is associated with the claim that substantial regional differences have been present in Christianity from the beginning. The Catholic historian, John Tracy Ellis, wrote *American Catholicism* (1956) to provide a widely read regional history of the Catholic Church in America. A second Catholic historian, Jay Dolan, went further in *The American Catholic Experience* (1985) in which he argues that tendencies toward the formation of an American Catholic Church within the Roman Catholic Church were present from the earliest period. The development of Catholicism in California is often neglected in histories of American Catholicism. James Hennesy, S.J., provides an important exception with his *American Catholics: A History of the Roman Catholic Community in the United States* (1981).

Catholic history in California begins with the entrance of Portolá and Serra. A companion of Serra's, Francisco Palou, O.F.M., left the definitive history of this entry and California history down to 1784 in his *Relación Histórica de la Vida y Apostólicas Tereas del Venerable Padre Junípero Serra* (1787). Maynard J. Geiger, O.F.M., provides a translation in *Palou's Life of Fray Junípero Serra* (1955). Portolá's second in command, Pedro Fages, also left a description of the earliest march from San Diego to Monterey in *A Historical, Political, and Natural Description of California,* translated by Herbert Ingram Priestly.

In the late nineteenth century, Hubert Howe Bancroft and his team of historians published the seven-volume *History of California* (1884-1890) as part of their monumental survey of the development of the West. The basic documents supporting this research are on file in the Bancroft Library at the University of California at Berkeley. Zephyrin Engelhardt, O.F.M., published *The Franciscans in California* (1897) in an effort to correct what he considered to be a distorted presentation by Bancroft of the Franciscan efforts in the mission period. He subsequently expanded his research and published separate histories of many of the missions.

Alfred Robinson, in his *Life in California* (1846), based on his experiences in the territory beginning in 1829, presents a detailed description of Southern California near the close of the mission period. Many editions of this work also include *Chinigchinich* by Father Gerónimo Boscana, translated by Robinson. It is an historic account of the Native Americans of California, particularly in the San Juan Capistrano area.

The forces behind the secularization of the missions and their subsequent collapse remain a controversial issue, partly because of widespread dissemination of romanticized "histories." C. Alan Hutchinson, in *Frontier Settlement in Mexican California* (1969), provides meticulous research based on examination of documents in Mexico City, which show that the Mexican government intended to turn over the mission lands to colonists sent north from Mexico. J.M. Guinn, in his *A History of California* (1915), collects original records including Mexican land grants which detail the struggle by the *Californios* for the mission lands in the period between the secularization of the missions and California statehood. In *Francisco Diego García, California's Transition Bishop* (1971), Msgr. Francis J. Weber provides a history of the Catholic Church during this period which saw the dissolution of the missions.

The role of the missions as part of the California Myth constitutes a portion of their history. Charles F. Lummis, a popular writer on the culture of the Spanish and Mexican periods, situates the California missions in the larger strategy of the Southwest in *The Spanish Pioneers and the California Missions* (1929). Kevin Starr includes consideration of them in *Americans and the California Dream, 1850-1915* (1973), his study of California as a regional culture, as well as in *Inventing the Dream: California through the Progressive Era* (1985). Interestingly, what Herbert Bishop Vaughan describes as "unblushing naturalism," Starr describes as a "sensual voluptuousness" which "did not encourage a sense of need for regeneration."

With statehood, American Catholicism supplanted Spanish Catholicism as the most influential regional form of Roman Catholicism. Francis J. Weber, archivist for the Archdiocese of Los Angeles, provides an important collection of materials for this, as well as the earlier and later periods, in his *Documents of California Catholic History* (1965). He also provides a comprehensive bibliography of sources in *A Select Guide to California Catholic History* (1966). Henry L. Walsh, S.J., in *Hallowed Were the Gold Dust Trails* (1946), describes the contributions of the English-speaking Irish missionaries to the developing pioneer towns of Northern California.

In post-Gold Rush California, Californian Catholicism shared in the development of American Catholicism. With accelerating immigration from Catholic countries, competition between various national groups became a central issue. R.A. Burchell provides an interesting overview of one of these groups in *The San Francisco Irish 1848-1880. The History of the Catholic Church in California* (1872) by William Gleeson is an interesting if not totally accurate product of this period which attempts to show, among other things, that the Irish arrived in America before the Spanish. *North Beach: The Italian Heart of San Francisco* (1985) by Richard Dillon provides an interesting narrative as well as excellent photographs by J.B.

Monaco of one of the Italian communities in San Francisco, while *From Italy to San Francisco* (1982) by Dino Cinel presents considerable research on the Italian immigrant experience.

Meanwhile in Southern California, Los Angeles developed more slowly, becoming for a time dominated by Protestants until political turmoil in Mexico early in the twentieth century again brought Catholic immigrants from south of the border. In *John Joseph Cantwell: His Excellency of Los Angeles* (1971), as well as in *Century of Fulfillment: The Roman Catholic Church in Southern California 1840-1947* (1990), Francis J. Weber provides detailed histories of the building of the Church during a period of unprecedented growth. Paul V. Murray, in volume one of *The Catholic Church in Mexico* (1965), details the history behind the later Hispanic immigrants which made them, at once, both devout and anti-clerical. John M. Ingham, in *Mary, Michael and Lucifer: Folk Catholicism in Central Mexico* (1986), presents an ethno-historical study of the folk Catholicism of the immigrants who came from predominantly central and southern Mexico rather than from Sonora, the origin of the earlier Mexican immigration.

Soon Catholic immigrants were arriving from all the countries of Central and South America. Penny Lernoux, in *People of God* (1989), provides a well-researched, journalistic study of post-Vatican II Catholicism in these countries. In *City of Quartz* (1990), Mike Davis includes a chapter on the Archdiocese of Los Angeles which focuses on political challenges to the hegemony and authority of the Church hierarchy in the increasingly Hispanic Catholic communities of Los Angeles.

Meanwhile, Catholics in Northern California were facing challenges of a different sort. In *The Documents of Vatican II* (1966), Walter M. Abbott, S.J., provides the basic material necessary for understanding the momentous changes brought about by the Second Vatican Council, conducted from 1962 to 1965. The new freedoms made possible by Vatican II coincided, in California, with the challenges to Catholic doctrine brought about by the human potential movement. In *Upstart Spring: Esalen and the American Awakening* (1983), Walter Truett Anderson provides a history of the Esalen Institute, a key institution in promoting that movement. David

Toolan, S.J., describes the impact made upon him by participation in the Esalen programs in the early seventies in *Facing West From California's Shores: A Jesuit's Journey Into the New Age Consciousness* (1987).

Part of the lure of Esalen involved the search for religious experience as an antidote for the pervasive secularism of the sixties conveyed in such works as *The Secular City* (1965) by Harvey Cox and by the Death of God philosophers. The secularism was allied with challenges to basic Church doctrine, such as those contained in *Honest To God* (1963) published by John A.T. Robinson, the Bishop of Woolwich in England.

The new freedom provided by Vatican II also provided an opportunity for long standing problems to surface. In March of 1966, Father James Kavanaugh wrote "I am a Priest, I want to Marry" for the *Saturday Evening Post*. The following year he published *A Modern Priest Looks at His Outdated Church* (1967) and *The Struggle of the Unbeliever* (1967), his dissertation, which he earlier had had to change to obtain the imprimatur.

Participation by Catholic clergy and members of the religious orders in California growth centers such as Esalen rapidly introduced new issues. William R. Coulson describes the impact of encounter workshops on the sisters of the Immaculate Heart Order in *Groups, Gimmicks and Instant Gurus: An Examination of Encounter Groups and their Distortions* (1972). In *The Jesuits: The Society of Jesus and the Betrayal of the Roman Catholic Church* (1987), Malachi Martin points out changes occurring in Jesuit circles at the same time.

In the early '70s Charles Y. Glock and Robert N. Bellah initiated a study of Bay Area groups and movements which they subsequently published as *The New Religious Consciousness* (1976). It included a consideration of the Catholic Charismatic Renewal, which is given fuller treatment by Kilian McDonell in *The Holy Spirit and Power* (1975) and *Charismatic Renewal and the Churches* (1976). Helen Tworkov also considered the Bay Area of this period in *Zen in America* (1989).

In 1973, a series of lectures were presented in San Francisco, subsequently published in *Sacred Tradition and Present Need* (1975) by Jacob Needleman and Dennis Lewis, which includes papers by William Johnston, S.J., speaking on "Christianity in Dialogue with

Zen" and Dom Aelred Graham speaking on "Contemplative Christianity." These marked the beginning of a resurgence of interest in
Catholic mysticism to which Brother David Steindl-Rast also contributed with "The Monk in Us," published in *Earth's Answer:
Explorations of Planetary Culture at the Lindisfarne Conferences* (1977),
edited by Michael Katz, William P. Marsh and Gail Gordon
Thompson. William McNamara, O.C.D., joined in the discussion
with "Psychology and the Christian Mystical Tradition" in
Transpersonal Psychologies (1975) by Charles Tart. *Christian Monasticism* (1969) by David Knowles provides a widely used source for
understanding the history and development of monasticism.

By the eighties, interest in Catholic spirituality had broadened
and become more academic, as is evidenced in publications such as
Devotion to the Holy Spirit (1985) by Joseph P. Chinnici, O.F.M., part
of a series on sources of American spirituality being published by
the Paulist Press. Another contribution is *Modern Christian Spirituality: Methodological and Historical Essays* (1990), edited by Bradley C.
Hanson for the American Academy of Religion, which contains
"Spirituality in the Academy" by Sandra M. Schneiders, I.H.M.
Patricia Christian-Meyer in *Catholic America: Self-Renewal Centers
and Retreats* (1989) describes how persons in greatly increased numbers were discovering and deepening their Catholic spirituality at
retreat centers.

At the same time there was increased Catholic participation in
the historical critical study of biblical texts. Helmut Koester, in
*Introduction to the New Testament, Vol. II, History and Literature of
Early Christianity* (1982), provides a comprehensive overview of
current biblical scholarship. Edgar Hennecke and Wilhelm
Schneemelcher have collected basic documents related to it in their
two-volume *New Testament Apocrypha* (1959). The definitive work
on the gnostic library discovered in Egypt is *The Nag Hammadi
Library* (1977), edited by James M. Robinson and recently revised
(1988). A comprehensive consideration of gnosticism is found in
Gnosis: The Nature and History of Gnosticism (1983) by Kurt
Rudolph. There are many studies of the Qumran scrolls. Millard
Burrows wrote *The Dead Sea Scrolls* (1955) concerning the earliest
finds, and Theodor H. Gaster provided an early useful translation

in *The Dead Sea Scriptures: In English Translation* (1956). Many scholars have been waiting for the full release of the texts and fragments recently published by the Biblical Archaeology Society in two volumes.

The Historical Jesus: The Life of a Mediterranean Jewish Peasant (1991) by John Dominic Crossan is a detailed study which takes the most current scholarship into consideration. Published at about the same time, *The Catholic Myth: The Behavior and Beliefs of American Catholics* (1990) is an equally detailed study by the Catholic sociologist, Andrew M. Greeley, based on data collected and studied at the University of Chicago's National Opinion Research Center. The response of Rome to current challenges to Catholic belief and practice is considered in *Vatican Authority and American Catholic Dissent: The Curran Case and Its Consequences* (1987), edited by William May, a collection of papers which includes "The Magisterium and Theological Dissent" by Cardinal Roger Mahony of Los Angeles.

Bibliography

Abbott, S.J., Walter M. and Msgr. Joseph Gallagher. *The Documents of Vatican II: The Message and Meaning of the Ecumenical Council with Notes and Comments by Catholic, Protestant and Orthodox Authorities.* Introduction by Lawrence Cardinal Shehan. New York: Guild Press, 1966.

Acuna, Rodolfo F. *A Community under Siege: A Chronicle of Chicanos East of the Los Angeles River 1945-1975.* University of California Press, 1984.

Ahlstrom, Sydney. *A Religious History of the American People.* New York: Doubleday, 1975.

Anderson, Walter Truett. *Upstart Spring: Esalen and the American Awakening.* Reading, MA: Addison-Wesley, 1983.

Ashton, Joan. *Mother of All Nations: The Visitations of the Blessed Virgin Mary and Her Message for Today.* New York: Harper & Row, 1989.

Bancroft, Hubert Howe. *History of California.* San Francisco: The History Company, 1884–1890.

Bancroft, Hubert Howe. *California Pastoral.* San Francisco: The History Company, 1888.

Bolton, Herbert Eugene (ed). *Fray Juan Crespí: Missionary Explorer on the Pacific Coast 1769-1774.* Berkeley: University of California Press, 1927.

Brandes, Ray (Trs.). *The Costanso Narrative of the Portolá Expedition.* Newhall, CA: Hogarth Press, 1970.

Bauer, Walter. *Orthodoxy and Heresy in Earliest Christianity.* Edited by Robert Kraft and Gerhard Krodel. Philadelphia: Fortress Press, 1971.

Brown, Emily. *The Passion at Pascua.* Tucson, Arizona: Tucson Chamber of Commerce, 1941.

Brown, Peter. *The Cult of the Saints: Its Rise and Function in Latin Christianity.* Chicago: University of Chicago Press, 1981.

Bruneau, Thomas C.; Gabriel, Chester E., and Mooney, Mary. *The Catholic Church and Religions in Latin America.* McGill University, 1984.

Burchell, R.A. *The San Francisco Irish 1848-1880.* Berkeley: University of California Press, 1980.

Cabal, Latorre. *The Revolution of the Latin American Church.* Norman, OK: University of Oklahoma Press, 1961.

Campbell, Peter A., and McMahon, Edwin M. *Bio-Spirituality: Focusing as a Way to Grow.* Chicago: Loyola University Press, 1985.

Campbell, Robert, O.P. *Spectrum of Catholic Attitudes.* Milwaukee, WI: The Bruce Publishing Co., 1969.

Chapman, Charles E. *A History of California: The Spanish Period.* New York: Macmillan and Company, 1921.

Chinnici, Joseph P., O.F.M. *Devotion to the Holy Spirit in American Catholicism.* New York: Paulist Press, 1985.

Christian-Meyer, Patricia. *Catholic America: Self-Renewal Centers and Retreats.* Santa Fe, NM: John Muir Publications, 1989.

Cinel, Dino. *From Italy to San Francisco: The Immigrant Experience.* Stanford, CA.: Stanford University Press, 1982.

Cleland, Robert Glass. *From Wilderness to Empire.* Edited by Glen F. Dumke. New York: Alfred Knopf, 1959.

Cogley, John. *Catholic America.* New York: The Dial Press, 1973.

Cox, Harvey Gallagher. *The Secular City: Secularization and Urbanization in Theological Perspective.* New York: MacMillan, 1965.

Costeloe, Michael P. *Church and State in Independent Mexico. A Study of the Patronage Debate: 1821-1857.* London: Royal Historical Society, 1978.

Crossan, John Dominic. *The Historical Jesus: The Life of a Mediterranean Jewish Peasant.* San Francisco: Harper San Francisco, 1991.

Coulson, William R. *Groups, Gimmicks and Instant Gurus.* New York: Harper & Row, 1972.

Davis, Mike. *City of Quartz.* New York: Verso, 1990.

Deedy, John. *American Catholicism: And Now Where?* New York: Plenum Press, 1987.

Delkin, James Ladd. *Monterey Peninsula.* California Writer's Project. Berkeley, CA: Courier Press, 1941.

Devine, George. *American Catholicism: Where Do We Go From Here?* Englewood Cliffs, NJ: Prentice-Hall, 1975.

Dillon, Richard. *North Beach: The Italian Heart of San Francisco.* San Francisco: Presidio Press. 1985.

Dolan, Jay P. *The American Catholic Experience,* New York: Doubleday, 1985.

Ellis, John Tracy. *American Catholicism.* University of Chicago Press, 1956.

Engelhardt, Zephyrin, O.F.M. *The Franciscans in California.* Harbor Springs, MI: Holy Childhood Native American School, 1897.

Eusibius. *The History of the Church: From Christ to Constantine.* Translated by G.A.Williamson. Minneapolis, Minn.: Augsburg Publishing House, 1975.

Fages, Pedro. *A Historical, Political, and Natural Description of California,* translated by Herbert Ingram Priestly. Berkeley: University of California Press, 1937.

Fallon, Timothy P., S.J. and Riley, Philip Boo. *Religion and Culture: Essays in Honor of Bernard Lonergan, S.J.* Albany: State University Press of New York, 1987.

Fox, Matthew. *The Coming of the Cosmic Christ.* Harper & Row, 1988.

Flynn, Maureen. *Sacred Charity.* Ithaca, N.Y.: Cornell University Press, 1989.

Gallagher, Charles A. and Maloney, George A.; Rousseau Mary F. and Wilczak, Paul F. *Embodied in Love: Sacramental Spirituality and Sexual Intimacy.* New York: Crossroad, 1983.

Geiger, Maynard J., O.F.M. *Palou's Life of Fray Junípero Serra.* Washington, D.C.: Academy of American Franciscan History, 1955.

Giles, Brother, O.F.M. *Yentou New Year: . . . A Life of Brother Benedict Jensen, Franciscan Missionary in China.* Oakland, CA: The Franciscan Fathers, 1959.

Gleeson, William. *History of the Catholic Church in California.* 2 volumes. San Francisco: A. L. Bancroft, 1872.

Glock, Charles Y., and Bellah, Robert N. *The New Religious Consciousness.* Berkeley: University of California Press, 1976.

Goergen, Donald J., O.P. *The Mission and Ministry of Jesus.* Wilmington, DE: Michael Glazier, 1986.

Greeley, Andrew M. *Come Blow Your Mind With Me.* New York: Doubleday, 1971.

_____. *The American Catholic: A Social Portrait.* New York: Basic Books, 1977.

_____. *The Catholic Myth: The Behavior and Beliefs of American Catholics.* New York: Charles Scribner's Sons, 1990.

Guinn, J. M. *A History of California and an Extended History of Los Angeles and Environs.* Los Angeles, CA.: Historic Record Co., 1915.

Hanna, Mary T. *Catholics and American Politics.* Cambridge: Harvard University Press, 1979.

Hanson, Bradley C. *Modern Christian Spirituality.* Atlanta, GA: Scholars Press, 1990.

Hanson, Harvey J. and Miller, Jeanne Thurlow. *Wild Oats in Eden.* Santa Rosa, CA: Hooper Printing, 1962.

Hardon, John A., S.J. *The Catholic Catechism: A Contemporary Catechism of the Teachings of the Catholic Church.* New York: Doubleday, 1981.

Hennesey, James, S.J. *American Catholics: A History of the Roman Catholic Community in the United States.* New York: Oxford University Press, 1981.

Hennecke, Edgar and Schneemelcher, Wilhelm. *New Testament Apocrypha. Vol. 1: Gospels and Related Writings.* English translation edited by R. Mclean Wilson. Philadelphia: The Westminster Press, 1959.

Hewett, Edgar Lee. *Ancient Life in the American Southwest*. Indianapolis, IN: Bobbs-Merrill, 1930.

Hitchcock, James. *The Decline and Fall of Radical Catholicism*. Herder and Herder, 1971.

Hutchinson, C. Alan. *Frontier Settlement in Mexican California: The Híjar-Padrés Colony, and Its Origins, 1769-1835*. New Haven: Yale University Press, 1969.

Ingham, John M. *Mary, Michael, and Lucifer: Folk Catholicism in Central Mexico*. Austin: University of Texas Press, 1986.

Katz, Michael; Marsh, William P. and Thompson, Gail Gordon. *Earth's Answer: Explorations of Planetary Culture at the Lindisfarne Conferences*. New York: Harper & Row, Lindisfarne Books: 1977.

Kavanaugh, James. *The Struggle of the Unbeliever*. New York: Trident Press, 1966.

Kavanaugh, James. *A Modern Priest Looks at his Outdated Church*. New York: Trident Press, 1967.

Kavanaugh, James. *Man in Search of God*. New York: Paulist Press, 1967.

Kelley, Francis Clement. *Blood Drenched Altars*. Milwaukee, WI: Bruce Publishing Company, 1935. (Revised Edition)

Kelly, Msgr. George A. *The Battle for the American Church*. New York: Doubleday, 1979.

Knowles, David. *Christian Monasticism*. New York: Mcgraw Hill, 1969.

Koester, Helmut. *History and Literature of Early Christianity*. Philadelphia: Fortress Press, 1982.

Landis, Benson Y. *The Roman Catholic Church in the United States: A Guide to Recent Developments*. New York: E.P. Dutton & Co., Inc. 1966.

Lernoux, Penny. *People of God: The Struggle for World Catholicism*. New York: Viking, 1989.

Levine, Daniel H. (ed.). *Religion and Political Conflict in Latin America*. Chapel Hill: University of North Carolina Press, 1986.

Lummis, Charles F. *The Spanish Pioneers and the California Missions*. Chicago: A.C. McClurg & Co., 1929.

Marett, R.H.K. *An Eye Witness of Mexico*. New York: Oxford University Press, 1939.

Martin, Malachi. *The Jesuits: The Society of Jesus and the Betrayal of the Roman Catholic Church*. New York: Simon and Schuster, 1987.

May, William W. (ed.). *Vatican Authority and American Catholic Dissent: The Curran Case and Its Consequences*. New York: Crossroad, 1987.

McAvoy, Thomas T., C.S.C. *The Americanist Heresy in Roman Catholicism: 1895-1900*. University of Notre Dame Press, 1963.

McDonnell, Kilian, O.S.B. *Charismatic Renewal and the Churches*. New York: Seabury Press, 1976.

_____ (ed.). *The Holy Spirit and Power: The Catholic Charismatic Renewal*. New York: Doubleday, 1975.

Meinig, D. W. *Southwest: Three Peoples in Geographical Change 1600-1970*. New York: Oxford U. Press, 1971.

Merton, Thomas. *Mystics and Zen Masters*. New York: Farrar, Strauss and Giroux. 1967.

Merton, Thomas. *The Asian Journal of Thomas Merton.* Edited by Naomi Burton, Brother Patrick Hart, and James Laughlin. New York: New Directions Press, 1973.

Murray, Paul V. *The Catholic Church in Mexico,* Vol. I. Mexico, D.F.: Editorial E.P.M., 1965.

Muscatine, Doris. *Old San Francisco: From Early Days to the Earthquake.* New York: G. P. Putnam's Sons, 1975.

Needleman, Jacob, and Lewis, Dennis. *Sacred Tradition and Present Need.* New York: Viking Press, 1975.

____. *Lost Christianity.* New York: Doubleday, 1980.

Novak, Michael. *Belief and Unbelief: A Philosophy of Self-knowledge.* New York: MacMillan, 1965.

____. *Ascent of the Mountain, Flight of the Dove.* New York: Harper & Row, 1971.

O'Brien, Robert. *California Called Them: A Saga of Golden Days and Roaring Camps.* New York: McGraw-Hill, 1951.

O'Brien, Robert, and Shannon, Thomas A. *Renewing the Earth.* New York: Doubleday, 1977.

Ord, Angústias de la Guerra. *Occurrences in Hispanic California.* Translated and edited by Francis Price and William E. Ellison. Washington D.C.: Academy of American Franciscan History, 1956.

Pennington, M. Basil, O.C.S.O. *Mary Today.* New York: Doubleday, 1987.

Ribes, Andrés Pérez de. *My Life Among the Savage Nations of New Spain.* Translated by Thomas A. Robertson in condensed form. Los Angeles: Ward Ritchie Press, 1968.

Rios-Bustamante, Antonio and Castillo, Pedro. *An Illustrated History of Mexican Los Angeles 1781-1985.* Berkeley: University of California, 1986.

Robinson, Alfred. *Life in California.* Santa Barbara, CA: Peregrine Publishers, 1970. Includes Boscana's *Chinigchinich.*

Robinson, James M. *The Nag Hammadi Library.* New York: Harper & Row, 1977.

Robinson, John A. T. *Honest to God.* Philadephia: Westminster Press, 1963.

Rudolph, Kurt. *Gnosis.* Translation by Robert Mclean Wilson. San Francisco: Harper & Row, 1983.

Salitore, Edward V. California Information Almanac. *California: Past, Present, Future.* Lakewood, CA: Edward Salitore, 1973 edition.

Schwaller, John Frederick. *Origins of Church Wealth in Mexico. Ecclesiastical Revenues and Church Finances 1523-1600.* Albuquerque: University of New Mexico Press, 1985.

Sinetar, Marsha. *Ordinary People as Monks and Mystics.* New York: Paulist Press, 1986.

Sneck, William Joseph. *Charismatic Spiritual Gifts: A Phenomenological Analysis.* University Press of America, 1981.

Starr, Kevin. *Inventing the Dream: California through the Progressive Era.* New York: Oxford University Press, 1985.

Starr, Kevin. *Californians and the the Californian Dream: 1850-1915.* New York: Oxford University Press, 1975.

Stein, Arthur. *Seeds of the Seventies: Values, Work and Commitment in Post-Vietnam America.* Hanover, NH: University Press of New England, 1985.

Stone, Irving. *Men to Match My Mountains: The Opening of the Far West. 1840-1900.* New York: Doubleday, 1956.

Tart, Charles. *Transpersonal Psychologies.* New York: Harper & Row, 1975.

Toolan, David, S. J. *Facing West from California's Shores.* New York: Crossroad, 1987.

Tworkov, Helen. *Zen in America.* Berkeley, CA.: North Point Press, 1989.

Walsh, Henry L., S.J. *Hallowed Were the Gold Dust Trails.* University of Santa Clara Press, 1946.

Weber, Francis J. *California's Reluctant Prelate: The Life and Times of the Right Reverend Thaddeus Amat (1811-1878).* Los Angeles: Dawson Book Shop, 1964.

____. *Documents of California Catholic History.* Los Angeles: Dawsons Bookshop, 1965.

____. *Select Guide to California Catholic History.* Los Angeles: Westernlore Press, 1966.

____. *Francis Mora; Last of the Cataláns.* Los Angeles: Westernlore Press. 1967.

____. *John Joseph Cantwell.* Hong Kong: Cathay Press, Ltd., 1970.

____. *The Founding of the Puebla de Nuestra Señora de Los Ángeles: A Study in Historiography.* Los Angeles: Archdiocese of Los Angeles, 1970.

____. *Francisco Diego García, California's Transition Bishop.* Los Angeles: Dawsons Book Shop, 1971.

____. *John Joseph Cantwell; His Excellency of Los Angeles.* Hong Kong: Cathay Press, 1971.

____. *The Religious Heritage of Southern California: A Bicentennial Survey.* Los Angeles: Interreligious Council of Southern California, 1976.

____. *The Laurelwood Mission. A History of Santa Clara de Asís.* Los Angeles: Archdiocese of Los Angeles, 1980.

____. *Century of Fulfillment: The Roman Catholic Church in Southern California 1840-1947.* Mission Hills, CA.: The Archival Center, 1990.

Williams, Cyril G. *Tongues of the Spirit: A Study of Pentecostal Glossolalia and Related Phenomena.* Cardiff: University of Wales Press, 1981.

Wills, Garry. *Bare Ruined Choirs: Doubt, Prophecy and Radical Religion.* Dell, 1972.

Wuthnow, Robert. *Experimentation in American Religion.* Berkeley: University of California Press, 1978.

ARTICLES

Blair, Margaret A. "Meditation in the San Francisco Bay area," *Journal of Transpersonal Psychology*, 1970.

Boulton, Wayne. "The thoroughly modern mysticism of Matthew Fox." *The Christian Century*, April 25 1990.

Gabriel, Chester E. "Spiritism in Manaus: The cults and Catholicism," in Thomas C. Bruneau, Chester Gabriel and Mary Mooney, *The Catholic Church and Religion in Latin America*. McGill University Press, 1984.

Graham, Dom Aelred. "Contemplative Christianity," in Jacob Needleman and Dennis Lewis, *Sacred Tradition and Present Need*. Viking Press, 1975.

Harman, Willis W. "The new Copernican revolution." *Journal of Transpersonal Psychology*, 1969.

Huxley, Aldous. "Human potentialities," *Psychology Today*, May 1967.

Johnston, William, S.J. "Christianity in dialogue with Zen," in Jacob Needleman and Dennis Lewis, *Sacred Tradition and Present Need*. Viking Press, 1975.

Johnston, William, S.J.,"Renewal in mystical theology," in Timothy Fallon, S.J., and Philip Boo Riley, *Religon and Culture: Essays in Honor of Bernard Lonergan, S.J.* Albany: State University Press of New York, 1987.

Kavanaugh, James. (pseud. Father Stephen Nash) "I am a priest and I want to marry," *Saturday Evening Post*, March 1966.

Kavanaugh, James. "Religious hang-ups," *Psychology Today*, July 1967.

Mahony, Archbishop Roger M. "The Magisterium and theological dissent." Presentation at the University of Southern California, 16 October 1986, in William May, ed., *Vatican Authority and American Catholic Dissent: The Curran Case and its Consequences*. New York: Crossroad, 1987.

McNamara, William, O.C.D. "Psychology and the Christian mystical tradition," in Charles Tart, *Transpersonal Psychologies*, 1975.

Murphy, Michael. "The group phenomenon," *Psychology Today*, December 1967.

Pike, James. "Religion and rebellion," *Psychology Today*, August 1967.

Santa Sabina Center. "Brochure," "Programs," "Newsletter"

Schneiders, Sandra. "Spirituality in the academy," in Bradley C. Hanson, *Modern Christian Spirituality*, Atlanta, GA: Scholars Press, 1990.

Steindl-Rast, Brother David. "The monk in us," in *Earth's Answer: Explorations of Planetary Culture at the Lindisfarne Conferences* edited by Michael Katz, William P. Marsh, and Gail Gordon Thompson. New York: Harper & Row: Lindisfarne Books, 1977.

*

Catholic Encyclopedia

Catholic Almanac, 1991 edition. Felician Foy, O.F.M. editor. Huntington, Native Americana: Our Sunday Visitor Publishing Division, 1991.

Index